RELEASED

CHAPTERS OF ERIE

By *Charles Francis Adams, Jr.*
and Henry Adams

32491

HE
2791
E68
A21C

GREAT SEAL BOOKS

A Division of Cornell University Press

ITHACA, NEW YORK

CORNELL UNIVERSITY PRESS

LONDON: GEOFFREY CUMBERLEGE

OXFORD UNIVERSITY PRESS

First published as Great Seal Book
by Cornell University Press in 1956

Printed in the United States of
America by the Vail-Ballou Press,
Inc., Binghamton, New York

Prefatory Note

ULYSSES S. GRANT had been president but a few months when the effects of his character showed themselves to be, in the words of Henry Adams, "startling—astounding—terrifying." In Jay Gould's attempt to corner gold on September 24, 1869—that famous "Black Friday"—was evidence that linked malpractice in Wall Street with corruption in Washington. But neither the author of *The Education* nor his older brother Charles Francis, Jr., could have been much startled or astounded by the simple fact of scandal. Both had more than once witnessed and written about chicanery in government and in business. Henry had recently published articles examining the relation of government to private finance and had just completed a piece on civil service reform; Charles during the past year had written several articles on the American railroad system, two of which were "The Erie Railroad Row Considered as an Episode in Court" (*American Law Review*, October 1868) and "A Chapter of Erie" (*North American Review*, July 1869), both devoted specifically to the legal and moral complexities of the Erie Railway wars and the inseparable financial machinations of Jay Gould himself. What was not only startling and astounding but terrifying as well was less the fact than the extent of the operation, and less the extent than the implications.

It was because of the implications that the Adamses regarded the dramatic scandal as "Heaven-sent"; they "jumped at it," *The Education* recalls, "like a salmon at a fly." Despite the risk of libel suits and perhaps even physical injury—the Erie people were "not regarded as lambs"—here was an investigation to be made; here was public service to be rendered. Forsaking a quiet vacation in Quincy, Massachusetts, they set forth to interview New York financiers, to observe Congress, to spell out, in short, the terror. Henry undertook to study the gold conspiracy; Charles chose to round out his history of the railway. The result was the publication of Henry's "The New York Gold Conspiracy" in the *Westminister Review*, October 1870, and Charles's "An Erie Raid" in the *North American Review*, April 1871. Read in sequence with the earlier "A Chapter of Erie," which embodied the still earlier "The Erie Railroad Row," their articles told—and continue to tell—an important tale.

It is not only that the two Adamses were able to interview Jim Fisk in his Opera House stronghold and to enter the offices of the great on Wall Street that makes their tale important; nor is it that together they collected and organized the facts in a manner that later research was to supersede only in casual details. It was, rather, that they understood the implications that had excited them. They knew that there is nothing so soft as a hard fact—facts may be molded to suit even the Devil's quotations—and they saw significance in the facts they found. Concerned with the processes of history and the nature of man, they perceived and illuminated with philosophical insight and felicitous artistry the character of the American nation and its essentially dialectical development.

The United States was about to enter upon the stage of modern history. As Hegel had foreseen in *The Philosophy of History*, the history of the United States as an organized state would begin once the frontier was closed, once nature ceased to be the realm in which conflicts could be settled and "the members of the political body . . . [should] have begun to be pressed back upon each other." Moreover, until the Civil War had accelerated the forces making for a highly industrialized society, the nation had been nourishing contradictions inherent in Jefferson's presidency. Although Jefferson had accepted

vi

the Hamiltonian premise of the importance of the federal government, he had in theory—if not always in practice—brought into the executive office a point of view opposed to developing its powers. And Andrew Jackson not long after him had perpetuated the difficulty by providing a rallying point for those pioneer Democrats who, while fervently believing in the value of the Union, actively opposed the enlargement or strengthening of the national organization. Herbert Croly was at his most astute in *The Promise of American Life* when he noted that the Democrats "were national in feeling, but local and individualistic in ideas." The Civil War had then been in the largest sense but a necessary culmination of a basic conflict, for when sectional interests that could not be geographically restricted had resulted in a clash that sections alone could not solve, the issue had had to be whether the national government should become an active agent in behalf of specific causes or whether it should adopt the more negative position of the uncommitted, disinterested umpire. The victory of logic and the Union armies had made certain that by the time of Grant's presidency the national interest should be identified with the supremacy of the federal government. Henceforth, among ambitious men, it was to be not so much a matter of neutralizing Washington's power as a matter of wielding it for oneself. Business, along with cities and political parties, had to assume the size appropriate to new needs and new powers. If in Jefferson's time liberty's struggle with authority had constituted a tension between thesis and antithesis, the post-bellum synthesis in the form of large-scale organization in all realms was constituting a new thesis and, necessarily, generating a new antithesis. Although the thesis could bear many labels, perhaps it took an Adams to apply the most telling one—Cæsarism, nicely suggestive of the conditions and risks of institutionalized life. But, whether the Adamses were needed or not, when the tree fell in the forest they were there to hear it.

On another level, the chapters about Erie are important for revealing the neglected Charles Francis Adams, Jr., as an astute historical analyst and a masterly, often ironic narrator. In fact, he shows himself in many ways more penetrating than his more celebrated brother. The bon mots, the organizing ideas are largely his. One can understand how after years of public service as a railroad commissioner and experience as a railroad director he could declare that among all the successful men he had met "not one would I care to meet again . . . either in this world or the next." At the same time, Henry is never without interest, for although at this relatively early moment of his development he may subordinate the role of ideas to the traditional role of character, he has not yet abandoned the particulars of history for the glittering equations of universal causation that would explain all the particulars away. Yet the mind of either Adams provides insights into significant issues. An anonymous pamphlet of 1868 entitled *The Erie War* begins:

The Erie Controversy has two points of interest—a speculative one for Wall Street, and a permanent and vital one for all who desire, by reducing the cost of transportation, to lighten the burdens upon the poor, to increase the gains of the rich, and to add to the prosperity of our city by attracting to it, through highways economically constructed and prudently managed, the foreign and domestic trade of the country.

A comparison of such a beginning with the beginning of the chapters that follow here is perhaps the best introduction anyone can provide to the Adamses' accomplishment.

*   *   *

The text of the present volume is taken from the edition of *Chapters of Erie and Other Essays,* by Charles F. Adams, Jr., and Henry Adams, published by Henry Holt, New York, in 1886. Differing slightly from the original periodical form of the articles, the book contains the material as the authors apparently wished to preserve it. The principal editorial departure from the Holt edition has been to substitute numbered footnotes for footnotes announced by asterisks and daggers.

ROBERT H. ELIAS
Cornell University

Contents

Chapters of Erie

A Chapter of Erie

NOT a generation has passed away during the last six hundred years without cherishing a more or less earnest conviction that, through its efforts, something of the animal had been eliminated from the higher type of man. Probably, also, no generation has been wholly mistaken in nourishing this faith;—even the worst has in some way left the race of men on earth better in something than it found them. And yet it would not be difficult for another Rousseau to frame a very ingenious and plausible argument in support of the opposite view. Scratch a Russian, said the first Napoleon, and you will find a Cossack; call things by their right names, and it would be no difficult task to make the cunning civilization of the nineteenth century appear but as a hypocritical mask spread over the more honest brutality of the twelfth. Take, for instance, some of the cardinal vices and abuses of the imperfect past. Pirates are commonly supposed to have been battered and hung out of existence when the Barbary Powers and the Buccaneers of the Spanish Main had been finally dealt with. Yet freebooters are not extinct; they have only transferred their operations to the land, and conducted them in more or less accordance with the forms of law; until, at last, so great a proficiency have they attained, that the commerce of the world is more equally but far more heavily taxed in their behalf, than would ever have entered into their wildest hopes while, outside the law, they simply made all comers stand and deliver. Now, too, they no longer live in terror of the rope, skulking in the hiding-place of thieves, but flaunt themselves in the resorts of trade and fashion, and, disdaining such titles as once satisfied Ancient Pistol or Captain Macheath, they are even recognized as President This or Colonel That. A certain description of gambling, also, has ceased to be fashionable; it is years since Crockford's doors were closed, so that in this respect a victory is claimed for advancing civilization. Yet this claim would seem to be unfounded. Gambling is a business now where formerly it was a disreputable excitement. Cheating at cards was always disgraceful; transactions of a similar character under the euphemistic names of "operating," "cornering," and the like are not so regarded. Again, legislative bribery and corruption were, within recent memory, looked upon as antiquated misdemeanors, almost peculiar to the unenlightened period of Walpole and Fox, and their revival in the face of modern public opinion was thought to be impossible. In this regard at least a sad delusion was certainly entertained. Governments and ministries no longer buy the raw material of legislation;—at least not openly or with cash in hand. The same cannot be said of individuals and corporations; for they have of late not infrequently found the supply of legislators in the market even in excess of the demand. Judicial venality and ruffianism on the bench were not long since traditions of a remote past. Bacon was impeached, and Jeffries achieved an immortal infamy for offences against good morals and common decency which a self-satisfied civilization believed incompatible with modern development. Recent revelations have cast more than doubt upon the correctness even of this assumption.[1]

[1] See a very striking article entitled "The New York City Judiciary" in the North American Review for July, 1867. This paper, which, from its fearless denunciation of a class of judicial delinquencies which have since greatly increased both in frequency and in magnitude, attracted great attention when it was published, has been attributed to the pen of Mr. Thomas G. Shearman, of the New York bar.

No better illustration of the fantastic disguises which the worst and most familiar evils of history assume as they meet us in the actual movements of our own day could be afforded than was seen in the events attending what are known as the Erie wars of the year 1868. Beginning in February and lasting until December, raging fiercely in the late winter and spring, and dying away into a hollow truce at midsummer, only to revive into new and more vigorous life in the autumn, this strange conflict convulsed the money market, occupied the courts, agitated legislatures, and perplexed the country, throughout the entire year. These, too, were but its more direct and immediate manifestations. The remote political complications and financial disturbances occasioned by it would afford a curious illustration of the close intertwining of interests which now extends throughout the civilized world. The complete history of these proceedings cannot be written, for the end is not yet; indeed, such a history probably never will be written, and yet it is still more probable that the events it would record can never be quite forgotten. It was something new to see a knot of adventurers, men of broken fortune, without character and without credit, possess themselves of an artery of commerce more important than was ever the Appian Way, and make levies, not only upon it for their own emolument, but, through it, upon the whole business of a nation. Nor could it fail to be seen that this was by no means in itself an end, but rather only a beginning. No people can afford to glance at these things in the columns of the daily press, and then dismiss them from memory. For Americans they involve many questions;—they touch very nearly the foundations of common truth and honesty without which that healthy public opinion cannot exist which is the life's breath of our whole political system.

I

The history of the Erie Railway has been a checkered one. Chartered in 1832, and organized in 1833, the cost of its construction was then estimated at three millions of dollars, of which but one million were subscribed. By the time the first report was made the estimated cost had increased to six millions, and the work of construction was actually begun on the strength of stock subscriptions of a million and a half, and a loan of three millions from the State. In 1842 the estimated cost had increased to twelve millions and a half, and both means in hand and credit were wholly exhausted. Subscription-books were opened, but no names were entered in them; the city of New York was applied to, and refused a loan of its credit; again the legislature was besieged, but the aid from this quarter was now hampered with inadmissible conditions; accordingly work was suspended, and the property of the insolvent corporation passed into the hands of assignees. In 1845 the State came again to the rescue; it surrendered all claim to the three millions it had already lent to the company; and one half of their old subscriptions having been given up by the stockholders, and a new subscription of three millions raised, the whole property of the road was mortgaged for three millions more. At last, in 1851, eighteen years after its commencement, the road was opened from Lake Erie to tide-water. Its financial troubles had, however, as yet only begun, for in 1859 it could not meet the interest on its mortgages, and passed into the hands of a receiver. In 1861 an arrangement of interests was effected, and a new company was organized. The next year the old New York & Erie Railroad Company disappeared under a foreclosure of the fifth mortgage, and the present Erie Railway Company rose from its ashes. Meanwhile the original estimate of three millions had developed into an actual outlay of fifty millions; the 470 miles of track opened in 1842 had expanded into 773 miles in 1868; and the revenue, which the projectors had "confidently" estimated at something less than two millions in 1833, amounted to over five millions when the road passed into the hands of a receiver in 1859, and in 1865 reached the enormous sum of sixteen millions and a half. The road was, in truth, a magnificent enterprise, worthy to connect the great lakes with the great seaport of America. Scaling lofty mountain ranges,

4

running through fertile valleys and by the banks of broad rivers, connecting the Hudson, the Susquehanna, the St. Lawrence, and the Ohio, it stood forth a monument at once of engineering skill and of commercial enterprise.

The series of events in the Erie history which culminated in the struggle about to be narrated may be said to have had its origin some seventeen or eighteen years before, when Mr. Daniel Drew first made his appearance in the Board of Directors, where he remained down to the year 1868, generally holding also the office of treasurer of the corporation. Mr. Drew is what is known as a self-made man. Born in the year 1797, as a boy he drove cattle down from his native town of Carmel, in Putnam County, to the market of New York City, and, subsequently, was for years proprietor of the Bull's Head Tavern. Like his contemporary, and ally or opponent,—as the case might be,—Cornelius Vanderbilt, he built up his fortunes in the steamboat interest, and subsequently extended his operations over the rapidly developing railroad system. Shrewd, unscrupulous, and very illiterate,—a strange combination of superstition and faithlessness, of daring and timidity,—often good-natured and sometimes generous,—he ever regarded his fiduciary position of director in a railroad as a means of manipulating its stock for his own advantage. For years he had been the leading bear of Wall Street, and his favorite haunts were the secret recesses of Erie. As treasurer of that corporation, he had, in its frequently recurring hours of need, advanced it sums which it could not have obtained elsewhere, and the obtaining of which was a necessity. He had been at once a good friend of the road and the worst enemy it had as yet known. His management of his favorite stock had been cunning and recondite, and his ways inscrutable. Those who sought to follow him, and those who sought to oppose him, alike found food for sad reflection; until at last he won for himself the expressive *sobriquet* of the Speculative Director. Sometimes, though rarely, he suffered greatly in the complications of Wall Street; more frequently he inflicted severe damage upon others. On the whole, however, his fortunes had greatly prospered, and the outbreak of the Erie war found him the actual possessor of some millions, and the reputed possessor of many more.

In the spring of 1866 Mr. Drew's manipulations of Erie culminated in an operation which was at the time regarded as a masterpiece; subsequent experience has, however, so improved upon it that it is now looked upon as an ordinary and inartistic piece of what is called "railroad financiering," a class of operations formerly known by a more opprobrious name. The stock of the road was then selling at about 95, and the corporation was, as usual, in debt, and in pressing need of money. As usual, also, it resorted to its treasurer. Mr. Drew stood ready to make the desired advances—upon security. Some twenty-eight thousand shares of its own authorized stock, which had never been issued, were at the time in the hands of the company, which also claimed, under the statutes of New York, the right of raising money by the issue of bonds, convertible, at the option of the holder, into stock. The twenty-eight thousand unissued shares, and bonds for three millions of dollars, convertible into stock, were placed by the company in the hands of its treasurer, as security for a cash loan of $3,500,000. The negotiation had been quietly effected, and Mr. Drew's campaign now opened. Once more he was short of Erie. While Erie was buoyant,—while it steadily approximated to par,—while speculation was rampant, and that outside public, the delight and the prey of Wall Street, was gradually drawn in by the fascination of amassing wealth without labor,—quietly and stealthily, through his agents and brokers, the grave, desponding operator was daily concluding his contracts for the future delivery of stock at current prices. At last the hour had come. Erie was rising, Erie was scarce, the great bear had many contracts to fulfil, and where was he to find the stock? His victims were not kept long in suspense. Mr. Treasurer Drew laid his hands upon his collateral. In an instant the bonds for three millions were converted into an equivalent amount of capital stock, and fifty-eight thousand shares, dumped, as it were, by the cart-load in Broad Street, made Erie as plenty as even Drew could desire. Before the astonished bulls could rally their faculties, the quotations had fallen from 95 to 50, and they realized that they were hopelessly entrapped.[2]

The whole transaction, of course, was in no respect more creditable than any result, supposed to be one of chance or skill, which, in fact, is made to depend upon the sorting of a pack of cards, the dosing of a race-horse, or the selling out of his powers by a "walkist." But the gambler, the patron of the turf, or the pedestrian represents, as a rule, himself alone, and his character is generally so well understood as to be a warning to all the world. The case of the treasurer of a great corporation is different. He occupies a fiduciary position. He is a trustee,— a guardian. Vast interests are confided to his care; every shareholder of the corporation is his ward; if it is a railroad, the community itself is his *cestui que trust*. But passing events, ac-

[2] A bull, in the slang of the stock exchange, is one who endeavors to increase the market price of stocks, as a bear endeavors to depress it. The bull is supposed to toss the thing up with his horns, and the bear to drag it down with his claws. The vast majority of stock operations are pure gambling transactions. One man agrees to deliver, at some future time, property which he has not got, to another man who does not care to own it. It is only one way of betting on the price at the time when the delivery should be made; if the price rises in the mean while, the bear pays to the bull the difference between the price agreed upon and the price to which the property has risen; if it falls, he receives the difference from the bull. All operations, as they are termed, of the stock exchange are directed to this depression or elevation of stocks, with a view to the settlement of differences. A "pool" is a mere combination of men contributing money to be used to this end, and a "corner" is a result arrived at when one combination of gamblers, secretly holding the whole or greater part of any stock or species of property, induces another combination to agree to deliver a large further quantity at some future time. When the time arrives, the second combination, if the corner succeeds, suddenly finds itself unable to buy the amount of the stock or property necessary to enable it to fulfil its contracts, and the first combination fixes at its own will the price at which differences must be settled. The corner fails or is broken, when those who agree to deliver succeed in procuring the stock or property, and fulfilling their contracts. The *argot* of the exchange is, however, a language by itself, and very difficult of explanation to the wholly uninitiated. It can only be said that all combinations of interests and manipulations of values are mere weapons in the hands of bulls and bears for elevating or depressing values, with a view to the payment of differences.

7

cumulating more thickly with every year, have thoroughly corrupted the public morals on this subject. A directorship in certain great corporations has come to be regarded as a situation in which to make a fortune, the possession of which is no longer dishonorable. The method of accumulation is both simple and safe. It consists in giving contracts as a trustee to one's self as an individual, or in speculating in the property of one's *cestui que trust*, or in using the funds confided to one's charge, as treasurer or otherwise, to gamble with the real owners of those funds for their own property, and that with cards packed in advance. The wards themselves expect their guardians to throw the dice against them for their own property, and are surprised, as well as gratified, if the dice are not loaded. These proceedings, too, are looked upon as hardly reprehensible, yet they strike at the very foundation of existing society. The theory of representation, whether in politics or in business, is of the essence of modern development. Our whole system rests upon the sanctity of the fiduciary relations. Whoever betrays them, a director of a railroad no less than a member of Congress or the trustee of an orphans' asylum, is the common enemy of every man, woman, and child who lives under representative government. The unscrupulous director is far less entitled to mercy than the ordinary gambler, combining as he does the character of the traitor with the acts of the thief.

No acute moral sensibility on this point, however, has for some years troubled Wall Street, nor, indeed, the country at large. As a result of the transaction of 1866, Mr. Drew was looked upon as having effected a surprisingly clever operation, and he retired from the field hated, feared, wealthy, and admired. This episode of Wall Street history took its place as a brilliant success beside the famous Prairie du Chien and Harlem "corners," and, but for subsequent events, would soon have been forgotten. Its close connection, however, with more important though later incidents of Erie history seems likely to preserve its memory fresh. Great events were impending; a new man was looming up in the railroad world, introducing novel ideas and principles, and it could hardly be that the new and old would not come in conflict. Cornelius Vanderbilt, commonly known as Commodore Vanderbilt, was now developing his theory of the management of railroads.

Born in the year 1794, Vanderbilt was a somewhat older man than Drew. There are several points of resemblance in the early lives of the two men, and many points of curious contrast in their characters. Vanderbilt, like Drew, was born in very humble circumstances in the State of New York, and like him also received little education. He began life by ferrying passengers and produce from Staten Island to New York City. Subsequently, he too laid the foundation of his great fortune in the growing steamboat navigation, and likewise, in due course of time, transferred himself to the railroad interest. When at last, in 1868, the two came into collision as representatives of the old system of railroad management and of the new, they were each threescore and ten years of age, and had both been successful in the accumulation of millions, —Vanderbilt even more so than Drew. They were probably equally unscrupulous and equally selfish; but, while the cast of Drew's mind was sombre and bearish, Vanderbilt was gay and buoyant of temperament, little given to thoughts other than of this world, a lover of horses and of the good things of life. The first affects prayer-meetings, and the last is a devotee of whist. Drew, in Wall Street, is by temperament a bear, while Vanderbilt could hardly be other than a bull. Vanderbilt must be allowed to be by far the superior man of the two. Drew is astute and full of resources, and at all times a dangerous opponent; but Vanderbilt takes larger, more comprehensive views, and his mind has a vigorous grasp which that of Drew seems to want. While, in short, in a wider field, the one might have made himself a great and successful despot, the other would hardly have aspired beyond the control of the jobbing department of some corrupt government. Accordingly, while in Drew's connection with the railroad system his operations and manipulations evince no qualities calculated to excite even a vulgar admiration or respect, it is impossible to regard Vanderbilt's methods or aims without recognizing the magnitude of the man's ideas and conceding his abilities. He involuntarily excites feelings of admiration for himself and alarm for the public. His ambition is a great one. It seems to be nothing less than to make himself master in his own right of the great channels of communication which connect the city of New York with the interior of the continent, and to control them as his private property. Drew sought to carry to a mean perfection the old system of operating successfully from the confidential position of director, neither knowing anything nor caring anything for the railroad system, except in its connection with the movements of the stock exchange, and he succeeded in his object. Vanderbilt, on the other hand, as selfish, harder, and more dangerous, though less subtle, has by instinct, rather than by intellectual effort, seen the full magnitude of the system, and through it has sought to make himself a dictator in modern civilization, moving forward to this end step by step with a sort of pitiless energy which has seemed to have in it an element of fate. As trade now dominates the world, and railways dominate trade, his object has been to make himself the virtual master of all by making himself absolute lord of the railways. Had he begun his railroad operations with this end in view, complete failure would have been almost certainly his reward. Commencing as he did, however, with a comparatively insignificant objective point,—the cheap purchase of a bankrupt stock,—and developing his ideas as he advanced, his power and his reputation grew, until an end which at first it would have seemed madness to entertain became at last both natural and feasible.

Two great lines of railway traverse the State of New York and connect it with the West,—the Erie and the New York Central. The latter communicates with the city by a great river and by two railroads. To get these two roads—the Harlem and the Hudson River—under his own absolute control, and then, so far as the connection with the Central was concerned, to abolish the river, was Vanderbilt's immediate object. First making himself master of the Harlem road, he there learned his early lessons in railroad management, and picked up a fortune by the way. A few years ago Harlem had no value. As late as 1860 it sold for eight or nine dollars per share; and in January, 1863, when Vanderbilt had got the control, it had risen only to 30. By July of that year it stood at 92, and in August was suddenly raised by a "corner" to 179. The next year witnessed a similar operation. The stock which sold in January at less than 90 was settled for in June in the neighborhood of 285. On one of these occasions Mr. Drew is reported to have contributed a sum approaching half a million to his rival's wealth. More recently the stock had been floated at about 130. It was in the successful conduct of this first experiment that Vanderbilt showed his very manifest superiority over previous railroad managers. The Harlem was, after all, only a competing line, and competition was proverbially the rock ahead in all railroad enterprise. The success of Vanderbilt with the Harlem depended upon his getting rid of the competition of the Hudson River railroad. An ordinary manager would have resorted to contracts, which are never carried out, or to opposition, which is apt to be ruinous. Vanderbilt, on the contrary, put an end to competition by buying up the competing line. This he did at about par, and, in due course of time, the stock was sent up to 180. Thus his plans had developed by another step, while through a judicious course of financiering and watering and dividing, a new fortune had been secured by him. By this time Vanderbilt's reputation as a railroad manager—as one who earned dividends, created stock, and invented wealth—had become very great, and the managers of the Central brought that road to him, and asked him to do with it as he had done with the Harlem and Hudson River. He accepted the proffered charge, and now, probably, the possibilities of his position and the magnitude of the prize within his grasp at last dawned on his mind. Unconsciously to himself, working more wisely than he knew, he had developed to its logical conclusion one potent element of modern civilization.

Gravitation is the rule, and centralization the natural consequence, in society no less than in physics. Physically, morally, intellectually, in population, wealth, and intelligence, all things tend to concentration. One singular illustration of this law is almost entirely the growth of this century. Formerly, either governments, or individuals, or, at most, small combinations of individuals, were the originators of all great works of public utility. Within the present century only has democracy found its way through the representative system into the combinations of capital, small shareholders combining to carry out the most extensive enterprises. And yet already our great corporations are fast emancipating themselves from the State, or rather subjecting the State to their own control, while individual capitalists, who long ago abandoned the attempt to compete with them, will next seek to control them. In this dangerous path of centralization Vanderbilt has taken the latest step in advance. He has combined the natural power of the individual with the factitious power of the corporation. The famous "L'état, c'est moi" of Louis XIV. represents Vanderbilt's position in regard to his railroads. Unconsciously he has introduced Cæsarism into corporate life. He has, however, but pointed out the way which others will tread. The individual will hereafter be engrafted on the corporation,—democracy running its course, and resulting in imperialism; and Vanderbilt is but the precursor of a class of men who will wield within the State a power created by the State, but too great for its control. He is the founder of a dynasty.

From the moment Vanderbilt stepped into the management of the Central, but a single effort seemed necessary to give the new railroad king absolute control over the railroad system, and consequently over the commerce, of New York. By advancing only one step he could securely levy his tolls on the traffic of a continent. Nor could this step have seemed difficult to take. It was but to repeat with the Erie his successful operation with the Hudson River road. Not only was it a step easy to take, but here again, as so many times before, a new fortune seemed ready to drop into his hand. The Erie might well yield a not less golden harvest than the Central, Hudson River, or Harlem. There was indeed but one obstacle in the way,—the plan might not meet the views of the one man who at that time possessed the wealth, cunning, and combination of qualities which could defeat it, that man being the Speculative Director of the Erie,—Mr. Daniel Drew.

The New York Central passed into Vanderbilt's hands in the winter of 1866–67, and he marked the Erie for his own in the succeeding autumn. As the annual meeting of the corporation approached, three parties were found in the field contending for control of the road. One party was represented by Drew, and might be called the party in possession, that which had long ruled the Erie, and made it what it was,— the Scarlet Woman of Wall Street. Next came Vanderbilt, flushed with success, and bent upon fully gratifying his great instinct for developing imperialism in corporate life. Lastly, a faction made its appearance composed of some shrewd and ambitious Wall Street operators and of certain persons from Boston, who sustained for the occasion the novel character of railroad reformers. This party, it is needless to say, was as unscrupulous, and, as the result proved, as able as either of the others; it represented nothing but a raid made upon the Erie treasury in the interest of a thoroughly bankrupt New England corporation, of which its members had the control. The history of this corporation, known as the Boston, Hartford, & Erie Railroad,—a projected feeder and connection of the Erie,—would be one curious to read, though very difficult to write. Its name was synonymous with bankruptcy, litigation, fraud, and failure. If the Erie was of doubtful repute in Wall Street, the Boston, Hartford, & Erie had long been of worse than doubtful repute in State Street. Of late years, under able and persevering, if not scrupulous management, the bankrupt, moribund company had been slowly struggling into new life, and in the spring of 1867 it had obtained, under certain conditions, from the Commonwealth of Massachusetts, a subsidy in aid of the construction of its road. One of the conditions imposed obliged the corporation to raise a sum from other sources still larger than that granted by the State. Accordingly, those having the line in charge looked abroad for a victim, and fixed their eyes upon the Erie.

As the election day drew near, Erie was of course for sale. A controlling interest of stockholders stood ready to sell their proxies, with entire impartiality, to any of the three contending parties, or to any man who would pay the market price for them. Nay, more, the attorney of one of the contending parties, as it afterwards appeared, after an ineffectual effort to extort black mail, actually sold the proxies of his principal to another of the contestants, and his doing so seemed to excite mirth rather than surprise. Meanwhile the representatives of the Eastern interest played their part to admiration. Taking advantage of some Wall Street complications just then existing between Vanderbilt and Drew, they induced the former to ally himself with them, and the latter saw that his defeat was inevitable. Even at this time the Vanderbilt party contemplated having recourse, if necessary, to the courts, and a petition for an injunction had been prepared, setting forth the details of the "corner" of 1866. On the Sunday preceding the election Drew, in view of his impending defeat, called upon Vanderbilt. That gentleman, thereupon, very amicably read to him the legal documents prepared for his benefit; whereupon the ready treasurer at once turned about, and, having hitherto been hampering the Commodore by his bear operations, he now agreed to join hands with him in giving to the market a strong upward tendency. Meanwhile the other parties to the contest were not idle. At the same house, at a later hour in the day, Vanderbilt explained to the Eastern adventurers his new plan of operations, which included the continuance of Drew in his directorship. These gentlemen were puzzled, not to say confounded, by this sudden change of front. An explanation was demanded, some plain language followed, and the parties separated, leaving everything unsettled; but only to meet again at a later hour at the house of Drew. There Vanderbilt brought the new men to terms by proposing to Drew a bold *coup de main*, calculated to throw them entirely out of the direction. Before the parties separated that night a written agreement had been entered into, providing that, to save appearances, the new board should be elected without

Drew, but that immediately thereafter a vacancy should be created, and Drew chosen to fill it. He was therefore to go in as one of two directors in the Vanderbilt interest, that gentleman's nephew, Mr. Work, being the other.

This programme was faithfully carried out, and on the 2d of October Wall Street was at once astonished by the news of the defeat of the notorious leader of the bears, and bewildered by the immediate resignation of a member of the new board and the election of Drew in his place. Apparently he had given in his submission, the one obstacle to success was removed, and the ever-victorious Commodore had now but to close his fingers on his new prize. Virtual consolidation in the Vanderbilt interest seemed a foregone conclusion.

The reinstalment of Drew was followed by a period of hollow truce. A combination of capitalists, in pursuance of an arrangement already referred to, took advantage of this to transfer as much as possible of the spare cash of the "outside public" from its pockets to their own. A "pool" was formed, in view of the depressed condition of Erie, and Drew was left to manipulate the market for the advantage of those whom it might concern. The result of the Speculative Director's operations supplied a curious commentary on the ethics of the stock exchange, and made it questionable whether the ancient adage as to honor among a certain class in society is of universal application, or confined to its more persecuted members. One contributor to the "pool," in this instance, was Mr. ——, a friend of Vanderbilt. The ways of Mr. Drew were, as usual, past finding out; Mr. ——, however, grew impatient of waiting for the anticipated rise in Erie, and it occurred to him that, besides participating in the profits of the "pool," he might as well turn an honest penny by collateral operations on his own account, looking to the expected rise. Before embarking on his independent venture, however, he consulted Mr. Drew, it is said, who entirely declined to express any judgment as to the enterprise, but at the same time agreed to loan Mr. —— out of the "pool" any moneys he might require upon the security usual in such cases. Mr. —— availed himself of the means thus put at his disposal, and laid in a private stock of Erie. Still, however, the expected rise did not take place. Again he applied to Mr. Drew for information, but with no better success than before; and again, tempted by the cheapness of Erie, he borrowed further funds of the "pool," and made new purchases of stock. At last the long-continued depression of Erie aroused a dreadful suspicion in the bull operator, and inquiries were set on foot. He then discovered, to his astonishment and horror, that his stock had come to him through certain of the brokers of Mr. Drew. The members of the "pool" were at once called together, and Mr. Drew was appealed to on behalf of Mr. ——. It was suggested to him that it would be well to run Erie up to aid a confederate. Thereupon, with all the coolness imaginable, Mr. Drew announced that the "pool" had no Erie and wanted no Erie; that it had sold out its Erie and had realized large profits, which he now proposed to divide. Thereafter who could pretend to understand Daniel Drew? who could fail to appreciate the humors of Wall Street? The controller of the "pool" had actually lent the money of the "pool" to one of the members of the "pool," to enable him to buy up the stock of the "pool"; and having thus quietly saddled him with it, the controller proceeded to divide the profits, and calmly returned to the victim a portion of his own money as his share of the proceeds. Yet, strange to say, Mr. —— wholly failed to see the humorous side of the transaction, and actually feigned great indignation.

This, however, was a mere sportive interlude between the graver scenes of the drama. The real conflict was now impending. Commodore Vanderbilt stretched out his hand to grasp Erie. Erie was to be isolated and shut up within the limits of New York; it was to be given over, bound hand and foot, to the lord of the Central. To perfect this programme, the representatives of all the competing lines met, and a proposition was submitted to the Erie party looking to a practical consolidation on certain terms of the Pennsylvania Central, the Erie, and the New York Central, and a division among the contracting parties of all the earnings from the New York

City travel. A new illustration was thus to be afforded, at the expense of the trade and travel to and from the heart of a continent, of George Stephenson's famous aphorism, that where combination is possible competition is impossible. The Erie party, however, represented that their road earned more than half of the fund of which they were to receive only one third. They remonstrated and proposed modifications, but their opponents were inexorable. The terms were too hard; the conference led to no result; a ruinous competition seemed impending as the alternative to a fierce war of doubtful issue. Both parties now retired to their camps, and mustered their forces in preparation for the first overt act of hostility. They had not long to wait.

Vanderbilt was not accustomed to failure, and in this case the sense of treachery, the bitter consciousness of having been outwitted in the presence of all Wall Street, gave a peculiar sting to the rebuff. A long succession of victories had intensified his natural arrogance, and he was by no means disposed, even apart from the failure of his cherished plans, to sit down and nurse an impotent wrath in presence of an injured prestige. Foiled in intrigue, he must now have recourse to his favorite weapon,—the brute force of his millions. He therefore prepared to go out into Wall Street in his might, and to make himself master of the Erie, as before he had made himself master of the Hudson River road. The task in itself was one of magnitude. The volume of stock was immense; all of it was upon the street, and the necessary expenditure involved many millions of dollars. The peculiar difficulty of the task, however, lay in the fact that it had to be undertaken in the face of antagonists so bold, so subtle, so unscrupulous, so thoroughly acquainted with Erie, as well as so familiar with all the devices and tricks of fence of Wall Street, as were those who now stood ready to take up the gage which the Commodore so arrogantly threw down.

The first open hostilities took place on the 17th of February. For some time Wall Street had been agitated with forebodings of the coming hostilities, but not until that day was recourse had to the courts. Vanderbilt had two ends in view when he sought to avail himself of the processes of law. In the first place, Drew's long connection with Erie, and especially the unsettled transactions arising out of the famous corner of 1866, afforded admirable ground for annoying offensive operations; and, in the second place, these very proceedings, by throwing his opponent on the defensive, afforded an excellent cover for Vanderbilt's own transactions in Wall Street. It was essential to his success to corner Drew, but to corner Drew at all was not easy, and to corner him in Erie was difficult indeed. Very recent experiences, of which Vanderbilt was fully informed, no less than the memories of 1866, had fully warned the public how manifold and ingenious were the expedients through which the cunning treasurer furnished himself with Erie, when the exigencies of his position demanded fresh supplies. It was, therefore, very necessary for Vanderbilt that he should, while buying Erie with one hand in Wall Street, with the other close, so far as he could, that apparently inexhaustible spring from which such generous supplies of new stock were wont to flow. Accordingly, on the 17th of February, Mr. Frank Work, the only remaining representative of the Vanderbilt faction in the Erie direction, accompanied by Mr. Vanderbilt's attorneys, Messrs. Rapallo and Spenser, made his appearance before Judge Barnard, of the Supreme Court of New York, then sitting in chambers, and applied for an injunction against Treasurer Drew and his brother directors, of the Erie Railway, restraining them from the payment of interest or principal of the three and a half millions borrowed of the treasurer in 1866, as well as from releasing Drew from any liability or cause of action the company might have against him, pending an investigation of his accounts as treasurer; on the other hand, Drew was to be enjoined from taking any legal steps towards compelling a settlement. A temporary injunction was granted in accordance with the petition, and a further hearing was assigned for the 21st. Two days later, however,—on the 19th of the month, —without waiting for the result of the first attack, the same attorneys appeared again before Judge Barnard, and now in the name of the people, acting through the Attorney-General, petitioned for the removal from office of Treasurer Drew. The papers in the case set forth some of the difficulties which beset the Commodore, and exposed the existence of a new fountain of Erie stock. It appeared that there was a recently enacted statute of New York which authorized any railroad company to create and issue its own stock in exchange for the stock of any other road under lease to it. The petition then alleged that Mr. Drew and certain of his brother directors, had quietly possessed themselves of a worthless road connecting with the Erie, and called the Buffalo, Bradford, & Pittsburg Railroad, and had then, as occasion and their own exigencies required, proceeded to supply themselves with whatever Erie stock they wanted, by leasing their own road to the road of which they were directors, and then creating stock and issuing it to themselves, in exchange, under the authority vested in them by law. The uncontradicted history of this transaction, as subsequently set forth on the very doubtful authority of a leading Erie director, affords, indeed, a most happy illustration of brilliant railroad financiering, whether true in this case or not. The road, it was stated, cost the purchasers, as financiers, some $250,000; as proprietors, they then issued in its name bonds for two million dollars, payable to one of themselves, who now figured as trustee. This person, then, shifting his character, drew up, as counsel for both parties, a contract leasing this road to the Erie Railway for four hundred and ninety-nine years, the Erie agreeing to assume the bonds; reappearing in their original character of Erie directors, these gentlemen then ratified the lease, and thereafter it only remained for them to relapse into the rôle of financiers, and to divide the proceeds. All this was happily accomplished, and the Erie Railway lost and some one gained $140,000 a year by the bargain. The skilful actors in this much-shifting drama probably proceeded on the familiar theory that exchange is no robbery; and the expedient was certainly ingenious.

Such is the story of this proceeding as told under oath by one who must have known the whole truth. That the facts are correctly set forth by no means follows. Indeed, many parts of this narrative are open to this criticism. The evidence on which it is founded may be sufficiently clear, but unfortunately the witnesses are not seldom wholly unworthy of credence. The formality of an oath may accompany plausible statements without giving to them the slightest additional weight. In this case the sworn allegations were made, and they implicated certain respectable men; it can only be said of them that their falsehood is not patent, and that they are thoroughly in character with other transactions known to be true. If the facts of the case were correctly stated, or had in them an element of truth, it is difficult to see what fiduciary relation these directors, as trustees, did not violate. However this may be, it is indisputable that the supply of Erie on the market had been largely increased from the source indicated, and Commodore Vanderbilt naturally desired to put some limit to the amount of the stock in existence, a majority of which he sought to control. Accordingly it was now further ordered by Mr. Justice Barnard that Mr. Drew should show cause on the 21st why the prayer of the petitioner should not be granted, and meanwhile he was temporarily suspended from his position as treasurer and director.

It was not until the 3d of March, however, that any decisive action was taken by Judge Barnard on either of the petitions before him. Even then, that in the name of the Attorney-General was postponed for final hearing until the 10th of the month; but, on the application of Work, an injunction was issued restraining the Erie board from any new issue of capital stock, by conversion of bonds or otherwise, in addition to the 251,058 shares appearing in the previous reports of the road, and forbidding the guaranty by the Erie of the bonds of any connecting line of road. While this last provision of the order was calculated to furnish food for thought to the Boston party, matter for meditation was supplied to Mr. Drew by other clauses, which specially forbade him, his agents, attorneys, or brokers, to have any transactions in Erie, or fulfil any of his contracts already entered into, until he had returned to the company sixty-eight thousand shares of capital stock, alleged to be the number involved in the unsettled transaction of 1866, and the more recent Buffalo, Bradford, & Pittsburg exchange. A final hearing was fixed for the 10th of March on both injunctions.

Things certainly did not now promise well for Treasurer Drew and the bear party. Vanderbilt and the bulls seemed to arrange everything to meet their own views; apparently they had but to ask and it was granted. If any virtue existed in the processes of law, if any authority was wielded by a New York court, it now seemed as if the very head of the bear faction must needs be converted into a bull in his own despite, and to his manifest ruin. He, in this hour of his trial, was to be forced by his triumphant opponent to make Erie scarce by returning into its treasury sixty-eight thousand shares,—one fourth of its whole capital stock of every description. So far from manufacturing fresh Erie and pouring it into the street, he was to be cornered by a writ, and forced to work his own ruin in obedience to an injunction. Appearances are, however, proverbially deceptive, and all depended on the assumption that some virtue did exist in the processes of law, and that some authority was wielded by a New York court. In spite of the threatening aspect of his affairs, it was very evident that the nerves of Mr. Drew and his associates were not seriously affected. Wall Street watched him with curiosity not unmingled with alarm; for this was a conflict of Titans. Hedged all around with orders of the court, suspended, enjoined, and threatened with all manner of unheard-of processes, with Vanderbilt's wealth standing like a lion in his path, and all Wall Street ready to turn upon him and rend him,—in presence of all these accumulated terrors of the court-room and of the exchange, the Speculative Director was not less speculative than was his wont. He seemed rushing on destruction. Day after day he pursued the same "short" [3] tactics; contract after contract was put out for the future

[3] An operator is said to be "short" when he has agreed to deliver that which he has not got. He wagers, in fact, on a fall.

delivery of stock at current prices, and this, too, in the face of a continually rising market. Evidently he did not yet consider himself at the end of his resources.

It was equally evident, however, that he had not much time to lose. It was now the 3d of March, and the anticipated "corner" might be looked for about the 10th. As usual, some light skirmishing took place as a prelude to the heavy shock of decisive battle. The Erie party very freely and openly expressed a decided lack of respect, and something approaching contempt, for the purity of that particular fragment of the judicial ermine which was supposed to adorn the person of Mr. Justice Barnard. They did not pretend to conceal their conviction that this magistrate was a piece of the Vanderbilt property, and they very plainly announced their intention of seeking for justice elsewhere. With this end in view they betook themselves to their own town of Binghamton, in the county of Broome, where they duly presented themselves before Mr. Justice Balcom, of the Supreme Court. The existing judicial system of New York divides the State into eight distinct districts, each of which has an independent Supreme Court of four judges, elected by the citizens of that district. The first district alone enjoys five judges, the fifth being the Judge Barnard already referred to. These local judges, however, are clothed with certain equity powers in actions commenced before them, which run throughout the State. As one subject of litigation, therefore, might affect many individuals, each of whom might initiate legal proceedings before any of the thirty-three judges; which judge, again, might forbid proceedings before any or all of the other judges, or issue a stay of proceedings in suits already commenced, and then proceed to make orders, to consolidate actions, and to issue process for contempt,—it was not improbable that, sooner or later, strange and disgraceful conflicts of authority would arise, and that the law would fall into contempt. Such a system can, in fact, be sustained only so long as co-ordinate judges use the delicate powers of equity with a careful regard to private rights and the dignity of the law, and therefore, more than any which has ever been devised, it calls for a high average of learning, dignity, and personal character in the occupants of the bench. When, therefore, the ermine of the judge is flung into the kennel of party politics and becomes a part of the spoils of political victory; when by any chance partisanship, brutality, and corruption become the qualities which especially recommend the successful aspirant to judicial honors, then the system described will be found to furnish peculiar facilities for the display of these characteristics.

Taking advantage of the occasion this system, so simple in theory, so complicated in practice, afforded for creating complications by obtaining conflicting orders from co-ordinate judges, the Erie party broke ground in a new suit. The injunction was no sooner asked of Judge Balcom than it was granted, and Mr. Frank Work, the Attorney-General, and all other parties litigant, were directed to show cause at Cortlandville on the 7th of March; and, meanwhile, Mr. Director Work, accused of being a spy in the councils of Erie, was temporarily suspended from his position, and all proceedings in the suits commenced before Judge Barnard were stayed. The moment, however, this order became known in New York, a new suit was commenced by the Vanderbilt interest in the name of Richard Schell; an urban judge cried check to the move of the rural judge, by forbidding any meeting of the Erie board, or the transaction of any business by it, unless Director Work was at full liberty to participate therein. The first move of the Drew faction did not seem likely to result in any signal advantage to its cause.

All this, however, was mere skirmishing, and now the decisive engagement was near at hand. The plans of the Erie ring were matured, and, if Commodore Vanderbilt wanted the stock of their road, they were prepared to let him have all he desired. As usual the Erie treasury was at this time deficient in funds. As usual, also, Daniel Drew stood ready to advance all the funds required—on proper security. One kind of security, and only one, the company was disposed at this time to offer,—its convertible bonds under a pledge of conversion.

The company could not issue stock outright, in any case, at less than par; its bonds bore interest, and were useless on the street; an issue of convertible bonds was another name for an issue of stock to be sold at market rates. The treasurer readily agreed to find a purchaser, and, in fact, he himself stood just then in pressing need of some scores of thousands of shares. Already at the meeting of the Board of Directors, on the 19th of February, a very deceptive account of the condition of the road, jockied out of the general superintendent, had been read and made public; the increased depot facilities, the projected double track, and the everlasting steel rails, had been made to do vigorous duty; and the board had, in the vaguest and most general language conceivable, clothed the Executive Committee with full power in the premises.[4] Im-

[4] This vote of the Board of Directors of the Erie Railway Company was the sole authority under which, without further consultation with the board, the stock of the road was increased four hundred and fifty thousand shares. It was worded as follows:—

"It being necessary for the finishing, completing, and operating the road of the company, to borrow money,

"*Resolved,* That under the provisions of the statute authorizing the loan of money for such purposes, the Executive Committee be authorized to borrow such sum as may be necessary, and to issue therefor such security as is provided for in such cases by the laws of this State; and that the president and secretary be authorized, under the seal of the company, to execute all needful and proper agreements and undertakings for such purpose."

The law referred to was Subdivision 10 of Section 28 of the General Railroad Act of 1850, which authorized the railroad companies to which it applied "to borrow such sums of money as may be necessary for completing, finishing, and operating the road"; to mortgage their roads as security for such loans; and to "confer on any holder of any bond issued for money borrowed as aforesaid, the right to convert the principal due or owing thereon into stock of said company, at any time, not exceeding ten years from the date of the bond, under such regulations as the directors may see fit to adopt."

It was an open question whether this law applied at all to the Erie Railway Company, the amount of the capital stock of which was otherwise regulated by law; the bonds were issued and sold, not as bonds, but with a distinct pledge of immediate conversion into stock, and as an indirect way of doing that, the direct doing of which was clearly illegal; finally, as a

24

mediately after the Board of Directors adjourned a meeting of the Executive Committee was held, and a vote to issue at once convertible bonds for ten millions gave a meaning to the very ambiguous language of the directors' resolve; and thus, when apparently on the very threshold of his final triumph, this mighty mass of one hundred thousand shares of new stock was hanging like an avalanche over the head of Vanderbilt.

The Executive Committee had voted to sell the entire amount of these bonds at not less than 72½. Five millions were placed upon the market at once, and Mr. Drew's broker became the purchaser, Mr. Drew giving him a written guaranty against loss, and being entitled to any profit. It was all done in ten minutes after the committee adjourned,—the bonds issued, their conversion into stock demanded and complied with, and certificates for fifty thousand shares deposited in the broker's safe, subject to the orders of Daniel Drew. There they remained until the 29th, when they were issued, on his requisition, to certain others of that gentleman's army of brokers, much as ammunition might be issued before a general engagement. Three days later came the Barnard injunction, and Erie suddenly rose in the market. Then it was determined to bring up the reserves and let the eager bulls have the other five millions. The history of this second issue was, in all respects, an episode worthy of Erie, and deserves minute relation. It was decided upon on the 3d, but before the bonds were converted Barnard's injunction had been served on every one connected with the Erie Road or with Daniel Drew. The 10th was the return day of the writ, but the Erie operators needed even less time for their deliberations. Monday, the 9th, was settled upon as the day upon which to defeat the impending "corner." The night of Saturday, the 7th, was a busy one in the Erie camp. While one set of counsel and clerks were preparing affidavits and

matter of fact, the proceeds of these bonds were not used for "completing, finishing, or operating the road." As a matter of law the question is of no interest outside of New York, and is as yet undecided there. Of the good faith and morality of the transaction but one opinion exists anywhere.

prayers for strange writs and injunctions, the enjoined vice-president of the road was busy at home signing certificates of stock, to be ready for instant use in case a modification of the injunction could be obtained, and another set of counsel was in immediate attendance on the leaders themselves. Mr. Groesbeck, the chief of the Drew brokers, being himself enjoined, secured elsewhere, after one or two failures, a purchaser of the bonds, and took him to the house of the Erie counsel, where Drew and other directors and brokers then were. There the terms of the nominal sale were agreed upon, and a contract was drawn up transferring the bonds to this man of straw, who in return gave Mr. Drew a full power of attorney to convert or otherwise dispose of the bonds, in the form of a promissory note for their purchase-money; Mr. Groesbeck, meanwhile, with the fear of injunctions before his eyes, prudently withdrew into the next room, and amused himself by looking at the curiosities and conversing with the lawyers' young gentlemen. After the contract was closed, the purchaser was asked to sign an affidavit setting forth his ownership of the bonds and the refusal of the corporation to convert them into stock in compliance with their contract, upon which affidavit it was in contemplation to seek from some justice a writ of *mandamus* to compel the Erie Railway to convert them, the necessary papers for such a proceeding being then in course of preparation elsewhere. This the purchaser declined to do. One of the lawyers present then said: "Well, you can make the demand now; here is Mr. Drew, the treasurer of the company, and Mr. Gould, one of the Executive Committee." In accordance with this suggestion a demand for the stock was then made, and, of course, at once refused; thereupon the scruples of the man of straw being all removed, the desired affidavit was signed. All business now being finished, the parties separated; the legal papers were ready, the convertible bonds had been disposed of, and the certificates of stock, for which they were to be exchanged, were signed in blank and ready for delivery.

Early Monday morning the Erie people were at work. Mr. Drew, the director and treasurer, had agreed to sell on that day fifty thousand shares of the stock, at 80, to the firms of which Mr. Fisk and Mr. Gould were members, these gentlemen also being Erie directors and members of the Executive Committee. The new certificates, made out in the names of these firms on Saturday night, were in the hands of the secretary of the company, who was strictly enjoined from allowing their issue. On Monday morning this official directed an employee of the road to carry these books of certificates from the West Street office of the company to the transfer clerk in Pine Street, and there to deliver them carefully. The messenger left the room, but immediately returned empty-handed, and informed the astonished secretary that Mr. Fisk had met him outside the door, taken from him the books of unissued certificates, and "run away with them." It was true;—one essential step towards conversion had been taken; the certificates of stock were beyond the control of an injunction. During the afternoon of the same day the convertible bonds were found upon the secretary's desk, where they had been placed by Mr. Belden, the partner in business of Director James Fisk, Jr.; the certificates were next seen in Broad Street.

Before launching the bolt thus provided, the conspirators had considered it not unadvisable to cover their proceedings, if they could, with some form of law. This probably was looked upon as an idle ceremony, but it could do no harm; and perhaps their next step was dictated by what has been called "a decent respect for the opinions of mankind," combined with a profound contempt for judges and courts of law.

Early on the morning of the 9th Judge Gilbert, a highly respected magistrate of the Second Judicial District, residing in Brooklyn, was waited upon by one of the Erie counsel, who desired to initiate before him a new suit in the Erie litigation, —this time, in the name of the Saturday evening purchaser of bonds and maker of affidavits. A writ of *mandamus* was asked for. This writ clearly did not lie in such a case; the magistrate very properly declined to grant it, and the only wonder is that counsel should have applied for it. New counsel were then hurriedly summoned, and a new petition, in a fresh name, was presented. This petition was for an injunction, in the name of Belden, the partner of Mr. Fisk, and the documents then and there presented were probably as eloquent an exposure as could possibly have been penned of the lamentable condition into which the once honored judiciary of New York had fallen. The petition alleged that some time in February certain persons, among whom was especially named George G. Barnard, —the justice of the Supreme Court of the First District,— had entered into a combination to speculate in the stock of the Erie Railway, and to use the process of the courts for the purpose of aiding their speculation; "and that, in furtherance of the plans of this combination," the actions in Work's name had been commenced before Barnard, who, the counsel asserted, was then issuing injunctions at the rate of half a dozen a day. It is impossible by any criticism to do justice to such audacity as this: the dumb silence of amazement is the only fitting commentary. Apparently, however, nothing that could be stated of his colleague across the river exceeded the belief of Judge Gilbert, for, after some trifling delays and a few objections on the part of the judge to the form of the desired order, the Erie counsel hurried away, and returned to New York with a new injunction, restraining all the parties to all the other suits from further proceedings, and from doing any acts in "furtherance of said conspiracy";—in one paragraph ordering the Erie directors, except Work, to continue in the discharge of their duties, in direct defiance of the injunction of one judge, and in the next, with an equal disregard of another judge, forbidding the directors to desist from converting bonds into stock. Judge Gilbert having, a few hours before signing this wonderful order, refused to issue a writ of *mandamus,* it may be proper to add that the process of equity here resorted to, compelling the performance of various acts, is of recent invention, and is known as a "mandatory injunction."

All was now ready. The Drew party were enjoined in every direction. One magistrate had forbidden them to move, and another magistrate had ordered them not to stand still. If the Erie board held meetings and transacted business, it violated one injunction; if it abstained from doing so, it violated another. By the further conversion of bonds into stock pains and penalties would be incurred at the hands of Judge Barnard; the refusal to convert would be an act of disobedience to Judge Gilbert. Strategically considered, the position could not be improved, and Mr. Drew and his friends were not the men to let the golden moment escape them. At once, before a new injunction could be obtained, even in New York, fifty thousand shares of new Erie stock were flung upon the market. That day Erie was buoyant,—Vanderbilt was purchasing. His agents caught at the new stock as eagerly as at the old, and the whole of it was absorbed before its origin was suspected, and almost without a falter in the price. Then the fresh certificates appeared, and the truth became known. Erie had that day opened at 80 and risen rapidly to 83, while its rise even to par was predicted; suddenly it faltered, fell off, and then dropped suddenly to 71. Wall Street had never been subjected to a greater shock, and the market reeled to and fro like a drunken man between these giants, as they hurled about shares by the tens of thousands, and money by the million. When night put an end to the conflict, Erie stood at 78, the shock of battle was over, and the astonished brokers drew breath as they waited for the events of the morrow. The attempted "corner" was a failure, and Drew was victorious,—no doubt existed on that point. The question now was, could Vanderbilt sustain himself? In spite of all his wealth, must he not go down before his cunning opponent?

The morning of the 11th found the Erie leaders still transacting business at the office of the corporation in West Street. It would seem that these gentlemen, in spite of the glaring contempt for the process of the courts of which they had been guilty, had made no arrangements for an orderly retreat beyond the jurisdiction of the tribunals they had set at defiance. They were speedily roused from their real or affected tranquillity by trustworthy intelligence that processes for contempt were already issued against them, and that their only chance of escape from incarceration lay in precipitate flight. At ten o'clock the astonished police saw a throng of panic-stricken railway directors—looking more like a frightened gang of thieves, disturbed in the division of their plunder, than like the wealthy representatives of a great corporation—rush head-long from the doors of the Erie office, and dash off in the direction of the Jersey ferry. In their hands were packages and files of papers, and their pockets were crammed with assets and securities. One individual bore away with him in a hackney-coach bales containing six millions of dollars in greenbacks. Other members of the board followed under cover of the night; some of them, not daring to expose themselves to the publicity of a ferry, attempted to cross in open boats concealed by the darkness and a March fog. Two directors, who lingered, were arrested; but a majority of the Executive Committee collected at the Erie Station in Jersey City, and there, free from any apprehension of Judge Barnard's pursuing wrath, proceeded to the transaction of business.

Meanwhile, on the other side of the river, Vanderbilt was struggling in the toils. As usual in these Wall Street operations, there was a grim humor in the situation. Had Vanderbilt failed to sustain the market, a financial collapse and panic must have ensued which would have sent him to the wall. He had sustained it, and had absorbed a hundred thousand shares of Erie. Thus when Drew retired to Jersey City he carried with him seven millions of his opponent's money, and the Commodore had freely supplied the enemy with the sinews of war. He had grasped at Erie for his own sake, and now his opponents derisively promised to rehabilitate and vivify the old road with the money he had furnished them, so as more effectually to compete with the lines which he already possessed. Nor was this all. Had they done as they loudly claimed they meant to do, Vanderbilt might have hugged himself in the faith that, after all, it was but a question of time, and the prize would come to him in the end. He, however, knew well enough that the most pressing need of the Erie people was money with which to fight him. With this he had now furnished them abundantly, and he must have felt that no scruples would prevent their use of it.

Vanderbilt had, however, little leisure to devote to the enjoyment of the humorous side of his position. The situation was alarming. His opponents had carried with them in their flight seven millions in currency, which were withdrawn from circulation. An artificial stringency was thus created in Wall Street, and, while money rose, stocks fell, and unusual margins were called in. Vanderbilt was carrying a fearful load, and the least want of confidence, the faintest sign of faltering, might well bring on a crash. He already had a hundred thousand shares of Erie, not one of which he could sell. He was liable at any time to be called upon to carry as much more as his opponents, skilled by long practice in the manufacture of the article, might see fit to produce. Opposed to him were men who scrupled at nothing, and who knew every in and out of the money market. With every look and every gesture anxiously scrutinized, a position more trying than his can hardly be conceived. It is not known from what source he drew the vast sums which enabled him to surmount his difficulties with such apparent ease. His nerve, however, stood him in at least as good stead as his financial resources. Like a great general, in the hour of trial he inspired confidence. While fighting for life he could "talk horse" and play whist. The manner in which he then emerged from his troubles, serene and confident, was as extraordinary as the financial resources he commanded.

Meanwhile, before turning to the tide of battle, which now swept away from the courts of law into the halls of legislation, there are two matters to be disposed of; the division of the spoils is to be recounted, and the old and useless lumber of conflict must be cleared away. The division of profits accruing to Mr. Treasurer Drew and his associate directors, acting as individuals, was a fit conclusion to the stock issue just described. The bonds for five millions, after their conversion, realized nearly four millions of dollars, of which $3,625,000 passed into the treasury of the company. The trustees of the stockholders had therefore in this case secured a profit for some one of $375,000. Confidence in the good faith of one's kind is very commendable, but possession is nine points of the law. Mr. James Fisk, Jr., through whom the sales were mainly effected, declined to make any payments in excess of the $3,625,000, until a division of profits was agreed upon. It seems that, by virtue of a paper signed by Mr. Drew as early as the 19th of February, Gould, Fisk, and others were entitled to one half the profits he should make "in certain transactions." What these transactions were, or whether the official action of Directors Gould and Fisk was in any way influenced by the signing of this document, does not appear. Mr. Fisk now gave Mr. Drew, in lieu of cash, his uncertified check for the surplus $375,000 remaining from this transaction, with stock as collateral amounting to about the half of that sum. With this settlement, and the redemption of the collateral, Mr. Drew was fain to be content. Seven months afterwards he still retained possession of the uncertified check, in the payment of which, if presented, he seemed to entertain no great confidence. Everything, however, showed conclusively the advantage of operating from interior lines. While the Erie treasury was once more replete, three of the persons who had been mainly instrumental in filling it had not suffered in the transaction. The treasurer was richer by $180,000 directly, and he himself only knew by how much more incidentally. In like manner his faithful adjutants had profited to an amount as much exceeding $60,000 each as their sagacity had led them to provide for.

The useless lumber of conflict, consisting chiefly of the numerous judges of the Supreme Court of New York and their conflicting processes of law, must next be disposed of. Judge Gilbert was soon out of the field. His process had done its work, and the Erie counsellors hardly deigned upon the 18th, which was the day fixed for showing cause, to go over to Brooklyn and listen to indignant denunciations on the part of their Vanderbilt brethren, as, with a very halting explanation of his hasty action, Judge Gilbert peremptorily denied the request for further delay, and refused to continue his injunction. It is due to this magistrate to say, that he is one of the most respected in the State of New York; and when that is said, much is implied in the facts already stated as to his opinion of some of his brother judges. Judicial demoralization can go no further. If Judge Gilbert was out of the fray, however, Judge Barnard was not. The wrath and indignation of this curious product of a system of elective judiciary cannot be described, nor were they capable of utterance. They took strange forms of expression. At one time he sent all the papers relating to the alleged conspiracy down to the grand jury, and apparently sought thereby to indicate that he courted an investigation. The prosecuting attorneys, however, better instructed in the law, seem to have doubted whether a matter which was the proper subject for a legislative impeachment could satisfactorily be brought before a petty jury on an indictment, and did not pursue the investigation. Then, at a later day, the judge mysteriously intimated that the belief of both the counsel and the affiants in the truth of the charges contained in the complaint before Judge Gilbert was then a matter of investigation before a criminal body, to see whether or not it constituted perjury. Finally, a heavy collection of counter-affidavits purified the judicial skirts from their taint, but not until fresh and more aggravated grounds for indignation had presented themselves. It is unnecessary to go into the details of the strange and revolting scenes which the next few months witnessed in the rooms of the Supreme Court. They read like some monstrous parody of the forms of law; some Saturnalia of bench and bar. The magistrate became more partisan than were the paid advocates before him, and all seemed to vie with one another in their efforts to bring their common profession into public contempt. Day and night detectives in the pay of suitors dogged the steps of the magistrate, and their sworn affidavits, filed in his own court, sought to implicate him in an attempt to kidnap Drew by means of armed ruffians, and to bring the fugitive by violence within reach of his process. Then, in retaliation, the judge openly

33

avowed from the bench that his spies had penetrated into the consultations of the litigants, and he astonished a witness by angrily interrogating him as to an affidavit reflecting upon himself, to which that witness had declined to make oath.[5] At one moment he wept, as counsel detailed before him the story of his own grievances and the insults to which he had been subjected, and then again he vindicated his purity by select specimens of pothouse rhetoric.[6] When the Vanderbilt counsel moved to fix a day on which their opponents should show cause why a receiver of the proceeds of the last over-

[5] *Question by the Court to Mr. Belden.* Did not Mr. Field send you, two or three days ago, an affidavit filled with gross abuse of me, and you declined to sign it?

Witness (producing a paper). This is the affidavit. I said I would rather not sign it. . . . .

Question by Mr. Field. Did you show that affidavit to Judge Barnard?

A. I did not.

Q. How, then, did he learn of its being sent to you?

Judge Barnard. He does not know, and never will in this world. I am now doing as other people have been doing; I have been followed by detectives for four or five weeks all over the city, and now I am following others. . . . .

Q. Was it not stated openly to you, in a law office below Chambers Street, that you must prevent, at all hazards, Judge Barnard from hearing this case?

A. In hearing which case, Judge? I do not know which case you refer to.

Q. The case before me. . . . .

Q. When you were present at the Metropolitan Hotel, did not one of the counsel, who was there, when he heard the complaint read, say that it was a shame to put Judge Barnard in as a defendant, and did not Dudley Field say, that by doing so he could frighten him off the bench and overawe the balance?

A. I do not remember anything of it.

Q. See if one of the counsel did not tell you that it was a shame to put him in as one of the defendants, and whether another of the counsel did not tell you that that was the only way to scare him off the bench, and that you could overawe the balance of the judges?

A. I don't remember anything being said about overawing any one.

[6] "In this wide city of a million or a million and a half of inhabitants, where a man can be hired for five dollars to swear any man's life away, there is not one so base as to come upon this stand and swear that I had anything to do with any conspiracy."

issue of stock should not be appointed, the judge astonished the petitions by outstripping their eagerness, and appointing Vanderbilt's own son-in-law receiver on the spot. Then followed a fierce altercation in court, in which bench and bar took equal part, and which closed with the not unusual threat of impeaching the presiding judge.[7] When Mr. John B. Haskin

[7] The matter before the court, regarding the bail of the contumacious directors, being disposed of, Mr. Clark, of the Vanderbilt counsel, rose and referred to another matter, which proved to be no less than an application for an order appointing a receiver of all the property, amounting to millions of dollars, which had been issued in violation of the injunction.

Mr. Field. This is an *ex parte* application and we do not care anything about it. The worse you make the case the better it will be in the end.

Mr. Rapallo. I ask your honor to make this order returnable on Monday morning.

The Court. I do not think it necessary to wait till Monday morning. You had better have it returnable forthwith.

Mr. Clark. We ask that that paper (the order to show cause instantly) be served upon Mr. Diven, who is now in court [. . .].

The order was then served on an individual director then in court, and Mr. Clark moved the appointment of the receiver.

Judge Barnard. Is there any objection to this application?

Mr. Field sat smiling in his chair, which was tipped back on its rear legs, and looked composed in the extreme, but made no response to the inquiry of the judge.

The Court. Draw up an order appointing George A. Osgood receiver of this fund, with security in the sum of $1,000,000, and requiring these defendants to appear before a referee in regard to the matter.

Mr. Field (rising). The court will understand that this was *ex parte*.

Mr. Clark. We have given notice, and therefore this is not *ex parte*.

Mr. Field. There has been no notice given; there has been no service. This is *ex parte,* and now if any one will enter that order, I want to see him do it.

Mr. Fullerton (excitedly and earnestly). I dare enter that order, and will do it with your honor's permission.

Mr. Field. May it please the court, there have been no papers submitted in this case, and no affidavits presented on which this order is made. You have made it upon blank paper, and in complete absence of any regular proceeding whatever. I wish to say, however, that just so sure as this proceeding is being taken in this form, a day of reckoning will as surely come, when these parties will have to answer before some one for this action.

Mr. Fullerton (in a decidedly animated tone). Let that day come, and

35

was placed upon the stand, there ensued a scene which Barnard himself not inaptly characterized the next day as "outrageous and scandalous, and insulting to the court." Upon this occasion the late Mr. James T. Brady seemed to be on the verge of a personal collision with the witness in open court; the purity of the presiding magistrate was impugned, his venality openly implied through a long cross-examination, and the witness acknowledged that he had himself in the course of his career undertaken for money to influence the mind of the judge privately "on the side of right." All the scandals of the practice of the law, and the private immoralities of lawyers, were dragged into the broad light of day; the whole system of favored counsel, of private argument, of referees, and of unblushing extortion, was freely discussed.[8] On a subsequent

---

there will be a reckoning that you will have to bear, and so will every one of those men who have been engaged in this transaction.

[8] John B. Haskin was called as the next witness for the people, and examined by Mr. Clark, and testified that he was an attorney at law, and had practised about twenty-six years.

Question by Mr. Clark. Were you ever employed by Mr. Dudley Field, professionally, prior to the 1st of March, or since?

A. I was applied to by Mr. Dudley Field, the attorney for Mr. Gould, on the 5th or 6th of March last, to accept a retainer in this Erie Railroad controversy, which I declined. I had never previous to that time been employed or requested to act as counsel by Mr. Field.

Mr. Brady, "on his own responsibility," objected to this line of examination; but after some discussion it was admitted, and the witness continued:—

Mr. Dudley Field, on the morning of the 5th or 6th of March, called at my office, and desired to retain me as counsel in this Erie controversy. I asked him on which side, and he said, "The Drew side." I asked him before whom, and he said, before Judge Barnard. I replied that my intimacy had been very great with Judge Barnard, and that I supposed he thought my influence as associate in this case would assist his side of the litigation.

Q. What further was said?

A. He said that he desired me to accept a retainer in the case, and said that if I would do so, it might be the means of avoiding serious trouble which would take place in the legislature, as I was Judge Barnard's friend, and if I would get that injunction modified I might, as his friend, prevent the terrible consequences which would result in this fight which was to

day the judge himself made inquiries as to a visit of two of
the directors to one gentleman supposed to have peculiar in-

---

take place, as Judge Barnard would be impeached; I then left him, and
went into another office. In a short time Dudley Field came back, and
handed me this book [producing a book], with his written modification of
the injunction, as I believe, in his own handwriting, saying, "If you will
get that signed by Judge Barnard, I will give you five thousand dollars; if
that sum is not sufficient, I will make it more." I declined the offer; and
having occasion to go to the City Hall to see Judge Barnard, I went, and
met him at the Astor House, where he had gone with some friends,—John
R. Hackett, Mr. Thomson, one of the directors of the Erie Railroad Company, and some others whom I do not recollect. I told him incidentally of
this application to me, and he said: "Dudley Field must be a dirty fellow
to apply to you for this modification in this way, for he applied to me in
court this morning for this same modification, and I refused to grant it."

Q. Did you see Dudley Field again?

A. I did not see him again.

Q. Did you accept the retainer?

A. I did not accept the retainer or undertake the service.

. . . .

Cross-examination by Mr. James T. Brady.

Q. Well, Mr. Haskin, have you ever in your life been applied to by
anybody, to use your influence, personally or professionally, with Judge
Barnard, to accomplish any result whatever?

A. Yes, sir; I think I have.

Q. Personally?

A. Yes.

Q. Professionally?

A. Yes.

Q. To influence his action as a judge?

A. Well, no; not that.

Q. What, then?

A. Well, in cases where there were great interests at stake, to point out
to him certain objects that were entitled to consideration.

Q. Did you ever agree or undertake to influence his action as a judge?

A. I might have done so on the side of right. What do you mean, sir?

Mr. Brady. O well, you will understand what I mean, sir. Have you never
in all your life used your influence with Judge Barnard to induce him to
make a decision in favor of some person in litigation whose cause you espoused?

A. I don't recollect any case of that kind.

Q. Will you swear that you have never done so?

fluence over the judicial mind, and evinced great familiarity with the negotiations then carried on, and even showed some

––––––––

A. I won't swear I didn't, because I might have done it in some case in the number of years I have been acquainted with him.

Q. Did you ever receive any kind of reward, directly or indirectly, for using any species of influence, or promising to use any species of influence, with Judge Barnard, or control or direct his action in any respect whatever?

A. I have never received anything; no, sir, except my legitimate fees, which I have received in references and so forth.

. . . .

He then asked him about his connection with the Christy will case.

Witness said he was general counsel in that.

Q. How did you earn your fee?

Witness. I will not answer; it is none of your business; it is impertinent.

Mr. Clark interposed, and said it was irrelevant.

Mr. Brady. I want to show that Mr. Haskin received a fee for his influence with the judge to gain a decision at the General Term.

Mr. Haskin said there was a suit pending about the matter.

Mr. Brady repeated that when he went into the case he knew the hostility with which he would be met. He was prepared for it. He had known some of the men a great many years, and he had hitherto kept still. He would repeat the question about the Christy will case.

Witness. I refuse to answer; it is none of your business.

Witness further on gave some testimony as to what he said to Judge Barnard about the Merchants' Express Company case before that judge last summer; he (witness) was not a counsel in it, but when on a fishing excursion last summer he was talking with the court about the law of the case. He told the judge there were some cases in which a judge could not afford to do a favor for a friend; I knew you were in the case, Mr. Brady; I told Judge Barnard that the newspapers were all down on the express monopoly.

Mr. Brady. Did you tell Judge Barnard in what cases a judge could afford to do a favor for a friend! You say you told him there were some in which a judge could not do a favor.

A. I did not say there were any.

. . . .

The next day it was supposed that Mr. Field would be examined and the court-room was crowded. Judge Barnard, however, declined to proceed any further, and ordered the evidence of the previous day to be stricken from the record. He further stated that he had already been busily engaged during the day in the other court-room, and did not intend to sit here to gratify impertinent curiosity. . . . . In regard to the examination of Mr. Field, he (Mr. Field) could make his affidavit *ex parte,* and would have disposition to extend the inquiry indefinitely into periodical literature.[9] Nor were the lawyers in any way behind the judge.

---

the same publicity given to his testimony as had been given to that taken yesterday.

Mr. Brady said he appeared this afternoon exclusively to attend to the examination of Mr. Field. Of course he had had no notice on his side of the case that there had been any conference between his honor and other eminent gentlemen as to what course should be taken. He had come to take charge of Mr. Field's case, and as regards whatever had happened, he took the whole responsibility of it. It belonged to him exclusively,—every question, every suggestion,—as it would also belong to him hereafter. He simply asked now that Mr. Field have the opportunity to be heard in the matter publicly, as the other witnesses had been.

Mr. Clark, in reply, said that he would give Mr. Brady a promise that, if he lived, he (Mr. Brady) should have the opportunity of examining Mr. Field before a referee, if they could agree upon a gentleman who should be acceptable.

.   .   .   .

Judge Barnard, in reply to Mr. Field, who asked for the appointment of a referee, said that he had made the only order in the case he would make today, and that the matter would now stand adjourned until Thursday next, at three o'clock, P. M.

No affidavit of Mr. Field was ever taken, and the subject was allowed to drop.

[9] *Question by the Judge to Mr. Belden.* Do you know whether James Fisk, Jr., and William H. Marston, went in a carriage to John J. Crane's house and offered him $50,000 to vacate this injunction; and did you hear from a director of the Erie Railroad that the Executive Committee had allowed that sum to be paid?

Answer. No one of the directors told me this; but I think I heard something of the kind. I can't tell from whom I heard it; there were numerous reports flying about at the time.

.   .   .   .

Judge Barnard. I haven't [addressing counsel] ruled the question out simply because I want to know whether I am fit to sit on the bench or not; if I have been engaged in a conspiracy, I am unfit to sit here.

Mr. Field said the question would open new evidence that had already been ruled out.

Judge Barnard. It was ruled out because I intend to have this "North American Review" [holding up the book] put in evidence, which contains an article about me, written by a clerk in your office. I intend to have this whole matter ferreted out.

39

At one moment they would indulge in personal wrangling, and accuse each other of the grossest malpractice, and the next, favor each other with remarks upon matters, more pointed than delicate. All this time injunctions were flying about like hail-stones; but the crowning injunction of all was issued, in reference to the appointment of a receiver, by Judge Clerke, a colleague of Judge Barnard, at the time sitting as a member of the Court of Appeals at Albany. The Gilbert injunction had gone, it might have seemed, sufficiently far, in enjoining Barnard the individual, while distinctly disavowing all reference to him in his judicial functions. Judge Clerke made no such exception. He enjoined the individual and he enjoined the judge; he forbade his making any order appointing a receiver, and he forbade the clerks of his court from entering it if it were made, and the receiver from accepting it if it were entered. The signing of this extraordinary order by any judge in his senses admits of no explanation. The Erie counsel served it upon Judge Barnard as he sat upon the bench, and, having done so, withdrew from the court-room; whereupon the judge immediately proceeded to vacate the order, and to appoint a receiver. This appointment was then entered by a clerk, who had also been enjoined, and the receiver was himself enjoined as soon as he could be caught. Finally the maze had become so intricate, and the whole litigation so evidently endless and aimless, that by a sort of agreement of parties, Judge Ingraham, another colleague of Judge Barnard, issued a final injunction of universal application, as it were, and to be held inviolable by common consent, under which proceedings were stayed, pending an appeal. It was high time. Judges were becoming very shy of anything connected with the name of Erie, and Judge McCunn had, in a lofty tone, informed counsel that he preferred to subject himself to the liability of a fine of a thousand dollars rather than, by issuing a writ of *habeas corpus,* allow his court "to have anything to do with the scandal."

The result of this extraordinary litigation may be summed up in a few words. It had two branches: one, the appointment of a receiver of the proceeds of the hundred thousand shares of stock issued in violation of an injunction; the other, the processes against the persons of the directors for a contempt of court. As for the receiver, every dollar of the money this officer was intended to receive was well known to be in New Jersey, beyond his reach. Why one party cared to insist on the appointment, or why the other party objected to it, is not very apparent. Mr. Osgood, the son-in-law of Vanderbilt, was appointed, and immediately enjoined from acting; subsequently he resigned, when Mr. Peter B. Sweeney, the head of the Tammany ring, was appointed in his place, without notice to the other side. Of course he had nothing to do, as there was nothing to be done, and so he was subsequently allowed by Judge Barnard $150,000 for his services. The contempt cases had even less result than that of the receivership. The settlement subsequently effected between the litigants seemed also to include the courts. The outraged majesty of the law, as represented in the person of Mr. Justice Barnard, was pacified, and everything was explained as having been said and done in a "Pickwickian sense"; so that, when the terms of peace had been arranged between the high contending parties, Barnard's roaring by degrees subsided, until he roared as gently as any sucking dove, and finally he ceased to roar at all. The penalty for violating an injunction in the manner described was fixed at the not unreasonable sum of ten dollars, except in the cases of Mr. Drew and certain of his more prominent associates; their contumacy his Honor held too gross to be estimated in money, and so they escaped without any punishment at all. Probably being as well read a lawyer as he was a dignified magistrate, Judge Barnard bore in mind, in imposing these penalties, that clause of the fundamental law which provides that "no excessive fines shall be imposed, or cruel or unusual punishments inflicted." The legal profession alone had cause to regret the cessation of this litigation; and, as the Erie counsel had $150,000 divided among them in fees, it may be presumed that even they were finally comforted. And all this took place in the court of that State over which the immortal Chancellor Kent had once presided. His great authority was still cited there, the halo which surrounds his name still shed a glory over the bench on which he had sat, and yet these, his immediate successors, could

> "On that high mountain cease to feed,
> And batten on this moor."

II

It is now necessary to return to the real field of operations, which had ceased on the morning of the 11th of March to be in the courts of law. As the arena widened the proceedings became more complicated and more difficult to trace, embracing as they did the legislatures of two States, neither of them famed for purity. In the first shock of the catastrophe it was actually believed that Commodore Vanderbilt contemplated a resort to open violence and acts of private war. There were intimations that a scheme had been matured for kidnapping certain of the Erie directors, including Mr. Drew, and bringing them by force within reach of Judge Barnard's process. It appeared that on the 16th of March some fifty individuals, subsequently described, in an affidavit filed for the special benefit of Mr. Justice Barnard, as "disorderly characters, commonly known as roughs," crossed by the Pavonia Ferry and took possession of the Erie depot. From their conversation and inquiries it was divined that they came intending to "copp" Mr. Drew, or, in plainer phraseology, to take him by force to New York; and that they expected to receive the sum of $50,000 as a reward for so doing. The exiles at once loudly charged Vanderbilt himself with originating this blundering scheme. They simulated intense alarm. From day to day new panics were started, until, on the 19th, Drew was secreted, a standing army was organized from the employees of the road, and a small navy equipped. The alarm spread through Jersey City; the militia was held in readiness;

in the evening the stores were closed and the citizens began to arm; while a garrison of about one hundred and twenty-five men intrenched themselves around the directors, in their hotel. On the 21st there was another alarm, and the fears of an attack continued, with lengthening intervals of quiet, until the 31st, when the guard was at last withdrawn. It is impossible to suppose that Vanderbilt ever had any knowledge of this ridiculous episode or of its cause, except through the press. A band of ruffians may have crossed the ferry, intending to kidnap Drew on speculation; but to suppose that the shrewd and energetic Commodore ever sent them to go gaping about a station, ignorant both of the person and the whereabouts of him they sought would be to impute to Vanderbilt at once a crime and a blunder. Such botching bears no trace of his clean handiwork.

The first serious effort of the Erie party was to intrench itself in New Jersey; and here it met with no opposition. A bill making the Erie Railway Company a corporation of New Jersey, with the same powers they enjoyed in New York, was hurried through the legislature in the space of two hours, and, after a little delay, signed by the Governor. The astonished citizens of the latter State saw their famous broad-gauge road thus metamorphosed before their eyes into a denizen of the kingdom of Camden and Amboy. Here was another dreadful hint to Wall Street. What further issues of stock might become legal under this charter, how the tenure of the present Board of Directors might be altered, what curious legal complications might arise, were questions more easily put than satisfactorily answered. The region of possibilities was considerably extended. The new act of incorporation, however, was but a precaution to secure for the directors of the Erie a retreat in case of need; the real field of conflict lay in the legislature of New York, and here Vanderbilt was first on the ground.

The corruption ingrained in the political system of New York City is supposed to have been steadily creeping into the legislature at Albany during several years past. The press has rung with charges of venality against members of this body; individuals have been pointed out as the recipients of large sums; men have certainly become rich during short terms in office; and, of all the rings which influence New York legislation, the railroad ring is currently supposed to be the most corrupt and corrupting. The mind of the unprejudiced inquirer, who honestly desires to ascertain the truth on this subject, will probably pass through several phases of belief before settling into conviction. In the first place, he will be overwhelmed by the broad, sweeping charges advanced in the columns of the press by responsible editors and well-informed correspondents. He will read with astonishment that legislation is controlled by cliques and is openly bought and sold; that the lobby is but the legislative broker's board, where votes are daily quoted; that sheep and bullocks are not more regularly in the market at Smithfield than Assemblymen and Senators at Albany. Amazed by such statements, the inquirer becomes incredulous, and demands evidence in support of them. This is never forthcoming. Committees of investigation—one or two in a session—are regularly appointed, and their reports are invariably calculated to confound the existing confusion. These committees generally express a belief in the existence of corruption and an utter inability to find it out; against some notoriously venal brother legislator they enter a Scotch verdict of "not proven"; and, having thus far been very guarded in their language, they then launch forth into tremendous denunciations of an unbridled and irresponsible press. Here they have it all their own way, and, indeed, too often make out an excellent case. Meanwhile the seeker after truth leaves both correspondents and committees, and tries to reach a conclusion by other means. Public rumor he finds to be merely a reflection of the press, or itself the impalpable form which the press reflects. No conviction can be had on such evidence. He finds loose statements, unproved assertions, and unsustained charges, tending to produce general incredulity. Where so much more is alleged than is proved, nothing is finally believed; until individual corruption may be almost measured by an ostentatious disregard of public opinion. Passing through the phase of incredulity, the inquirer may at last resort to the private judgment of the best informed. Appealing to individuals in whose purity, judicial temper, and means of information he has entire confidence, he will probably find his conclusions as discouraging as they are inevitable. The weight of opinion and of evidence gradually becomes irresistible, until his mind settles down into a sad belief that probably no representative bodies were ever more thoroughly venal, more shamelessly corrupt, or more hopelessly beyond the reach of public opinion, than are certain of those bodies which legislate for republican America in this latter half of the nineteenth century. Certainly, none of the developments which marked the Erie conflict in the New York legislature of 1868 would tend to throw doubts on this conclusion when once arrived at.

One favorite method of procedure at Albany is through the appointment of committees to investigate the affairs of wealthy corporations. The stock of some great company is manipulated till it fluctuates violently, as was the case with Pacific Mail in 1867. Forthwith some member of the Assembly rises and calls for a committee of investigation. The instant the game is afoot, a rush is made for positions on the committee. The proposer, of course, is a member, probably chairman. The advantages of the position are obvious. The committee constitutes a little temporary outside ring. If a member is corrupt, he has substantial advantages offered him to influence his action in regard to the report. If he is not open to bribery, he is nevertheless in possession of very valuable information, and an innocent little remark, casually let fall, may lead a son, a brother, or a loving cousin to make very judicious purchases of stock. Altogether, the position is one not to be avoided.

The investigation phase was the first which the Erie struggle assumed at Albany. During the early stages of the conflict the legislature had scented the carnage from afar. There was "money in it," and the struggle was watched with breathless interest. As early as the 5th of March the subject had been introduced into the State Senate, and an investigation into the circumstances of the company was called for. A committee of three was ordered, but the next day a senator, by name Mattoon, moved to increase the number to five, which was done, he himself being naturally one of the additional members. This committee had its first sitting on the 10th, at the very crisis of the great explosion. But before the investigation was entered upon, Mr. Mattoon thought it expedient to convince the contending parties of his own perfect impartiality and firm determination to hold in check the corrupt impulses of his associates. With this end in view, upon the 9th or the 10th he hurried down to New York, and visited West Street, where he had an interview with the leading Erie directors. He explained to them the corrupt motives which had led to the appointment of the committee, and how his sole object in obtaining an increase of the number had been to put himself in a position in which he might be able to prevent these evil practices and see fair play. Curiously enough, at the same interview he mentioned that his son was to be appointed an assistant sergeant-at-arms to aid in the investigation, and proved his disinterestedness by mentioning the fact that this son was to serve without pay. The labors of the committee continued until the 31st of March, and during that time Mr. Mattoon, and at least one other senator, pursued a course of private inquiry which involved further visits to Jersey City. Naturally enough, Mr. Drew and his associates took it into their heads that the man wanted to be bought, and even affirmed subsequently that, at one interview, he had in pretty broad terms offered himself for sale. It has not been distinctly stated in evidence by any one that an attempt was made on his purity or on that of his public-spirited son; and it is difficult to believe that one who came to New York so full of high purpose could have been sufficiently corrupted by metropolitan influences to receive bribes from both sides. Whether he did so or not his proceedings were terribly suggestive as regards legislative morality at Albany. Here was a senator, a member of a committee of investigation, rousing gamblers from their beds at early hours of the morning to hold interviews in the faro-bank parlor of the establishment, and to give "points" on which to operate upon the joint account. Even then the wretched creature could not even keep faith with his very "pals"; he wrote to them to "go it heavy" for Drew, and then himself went over to Vanderbilt,—he made agreements to share profits and then submitted to exposure sooner than meet his part of the loss. A man more thoroughly, shame-facedly contemptible and corrupt,—a more perfect specimen of a legislator on sale haggling for his own price, could not well exist. In this case he cheated every one, including himself. Accident threw great opportunities in his way. On the 31st the draft of a proposed report, exonerating in great measure the Drew faction, was read to him by an associate, to which he not only made no objection, but was even understood to assent. On the same day another report was read in his presence, strongly denouncing the Drew faction, sustaining to the fullest extent the charges made against it, and characterizing its conduct as corrupt and disgraceful. Each report was signed by two of his associates, and Mr. Mattoon found himself in the position of holding the balance of power; whichever report he signed would be the report of the committee. He expressed a desire to think the matter over. It is natural to suppose that, in his eagerness to gain information privately, Mr. Mattoon had not confined his unofficial visits to the Drew camp. In any case his mind was in a state of painful suspense. Finally, after arranging in consultation on Tuesday for a report favoring the Drew party, on Wednesday he signed a report strongly denouncing it, and by doing so settled the action of the committee. Mr. Jay Gould must have been acquainted with the circumstances of the case, and evidently supposed that Mr. Mattoon was "fixed," since he subsequently declared he was "astounded" when he heard that Mr. Mattoon had signed this report. The committee, however, with their patriotic sergeant-at-arms, whose services, by the way, cost the State but a hundred dollars, desisted at length from their labors, the result of which was one more point gained by Commodore Vanderbilt.

Indeed, Vanderbilt had thus far as much outgeneralled Drew in the manufacture of public opinion as Drew had outgeneralled Vanderbilt in the manufacture of Erie stock. His whole scheme was one of monopoly, which was opposed to every interest of the city and State of New York, yet into the support of this scheme he had brought all the leading papers of New York City, with a single exception. Now again he seemed to have it all his own way in the legislature, and the tide ran strongly against the exiles of Erie. The report of the investigation committee was signed on April 1st, and may be considered as marking the high-water point of Vanderbilt's success. Hitherto the Albany interests of the exiles had been confided to mere agents, and had not prospered; but, when fairly roused by a sense of danger, the Drew party showed at least as close a familiarity with the tactics of Albany as with those of Wall Street. The moment they felt themselves settled at Jersey City they had gone to work to excite a popular sympathy in their own behalf. The cry of monopoly was a sure card in their hands. They cared no more for the actual welfare of commerce, involved in railroad competition, than they did for the real interests of the Erie Railway; but they judged truly that there was no limit to the extent to which the public might be imposed upon. An active competition with the Vanderbilt roads, by land and water, was inaugurated; fares and freights on the Erie were reduced on an average by one third; sounding proclamations were issued; "interviewers" from the press returned rejoicing from Taylor's Hotel to New York City, and the Jersey shore quaked under the clatter of this Chinese battle. The influence of these tactics made itself felt at once. By the middle of March memorials against monopoly began to flow in at Albany.

While popular sympathy was thus roused by the bribe of active competition, a bill was introduced into the Assembly, in the Erie interest, legalizing the recent issue of new stock, declaring and regulating the power of issuing convertible bonds, providing for a broad-gauge connection with Chicago and the guaranty of the bonds of the Boston, Hartford, & Erie, and finally forbidding, in so far as any legislation could forbid, the consolidation of the Central and the Erie in the hands of Vanderbilt. This bill was referred to the Committee on Railroads on the 13th of March. On the 20th a public hearing was begun, and the committee proceeded to take evidence, aided by a long array of opposing counsel, most of whom had figured in the proceedings in the courts of law. In a few days the bill was adversely reported upon, and the report adopted in the Assembly by the decisive vote of eighty-three to thirty-two. This was upon the 27th of March. The hint was a broad one; the exiles must give closer attention to their interests. So soon as the news of this adverse action reached Jersey City, it was decided that Mr. Jay Gould should brave the terrors of the law, and personally superintend matters at Albany. Neither Mr. Drew nor his associates desired to become permanent residents of Jersey City; nor did they wish to return to New York as criminals on their way to jail. Mr. Gould was to pave the way to a different return by causing the recent issue of convertible bonds to be legalized. That once done, Commodore Vanderbilt was not the man to wage an unavailing war, and a compromise, in which Barnard and his processes of contempt would be thrown in as a make-weight, could easily be effected. A rumor was therefore started that Mr. Gould was to leave for Ohio, supplied with the necessary authority and funds to press vigorously to completion the eighty miles of broad-gauge track between Akron and Toledo, which would open to the Erie the much-coveted connection with Chicago. Having hung out this false light, Mr. Jay Gould went on his mission, the president of the company having some time previously drawn half a million of dollars out of the overflowing Erie treasury.

This mission was by no means unattended by difficulties. In the first place, Judge Barnard's processes for contempt seemed to threaten the liberty of Mr. Gould's person. He left Jersey City and arrived at Albany on the 30th day of March, three days after the defeat of the Erie bill, and two days before Mr. Mattoon had made up his mind as to which report he would sign. Naturally his opponents were well satisfied with the present aspect of affairs, and saw no benefit likely to arise from Mr. Gould's presence in Albany. The day after his arrival, therefore, he was arrested, on the writ issued against him for contempt of court, and held to bail in half a million of dollars for his appearance in New York on the following Saturday. He was immediately bailed of course, and for the next few days devoted himself assiduously to the business he had in hand. On Saturday he appeared before Judge Barnard, and was duly put in charge of the sheriff to answer certain interrogatories. It would seem to have been perfectly easy for him to give the necessary bail, and to return from Barnard's presence at once to Albany; but the simple method seems never to have been resorted to throughout these complications: nothing was ever done without the interposition of a writ and the assistance of a crowd of counsel. In this case Judge Barrett of the Common Pleas was appealed to, who issued a writ of *habeas corpus,* by virtue of which Mr. Gould was taken out of the hands of the sheriff and again brought into court. Of course the hearing of the case was deferred, and it was equally a matter of course that Mr. Gould was bent on returning at once to his field of labor. The officer to whose care Mr. Gould was intrusted was especially warned by the court, in Mr. Gould's presence, that he was not to allow his charge to go out of his sight. This difficulty was easily surmounted. Mr. Gould went by an early train to Albany, taking the officer with him in the capacity of a travelling companion. Once in Albany he was naturally taken ill,—not too ill to go to the Capitol in the midst of a snow-storm, but much too ill to think of returning to New York. On the 10th the trusty official and travelling companion signified to Mr. Gould that his presence was much desired before Judge Barrett, and intimated an intention of carrying him back to New York. Mr. Gould then pleaded the delicate condition of his health, and wholly declined to undergo the hardships of the proposed journey. Whereupon the officer, stimulated, as was alleged, by Gould's opponents, returned alone to New York, and reported his charge to the court as a runaway. A new spectacle of judicial indignation ensued, and a new process for contempt seemed imminent. Of course nothing came of it. A few affidavits from Albany pacified the indignant Barrett. The application for a *habeas corpus* was discharged, and Mr. Gould was theoretically returned into the custody of the sheriff. Thereupon the required security for his appearance when needed was given; and meanwhile, pending the recovery of his health, he assiduously devoted the tedious hours of convalescence to the task of cultivating a thorough understanding between himself and the members of the legislature.

A strange legislative episode occurred at this time, which for a day or two threatened to thwart Mr. Gould's operations, but in the end materially facilitated them. All through March the usual sensational charges had been flying through the press in relation to the buying of votes on the pending Erie measures. These were as vague and as difficult to sustain as usual, and it was very important that no indiscreet friend of legislative purity should blunder out charges which could be triumphantly refuted. On the 1st of April, however, the second day after Mr. Gould appeared on the ground, a quiet country member named Glenn, remarkable for nothing but his advanced years and white hair, suddenly created an intense sensation by rising in his place in the Assembly and excitedly declaring that he had just been offered money for his vote on the Erie Bill. He then sent up to the Speaker charges in writing, to the effect that the recent report on the bill in question was bought, that members of the House were engaged in purchasing votes, that reports of committees were habitually sold, and ended by charging "corruption, deep, dark, and damning on a portion of the House," of which he felt "degraded in being a member." A committee of investigation was, of course, appointed, and the press congratulated the public that at last specific charges had been advanced from a responsible quarter. On the 9th Mr. Glenn followed up the attack by charging, again in writing, that one member of the committee of investigation, whose name he gave, was the very member who had offered him money for his vote. Mr. Frear, the member in question, at once resigned his place upon the committee, and demanded an investigation. Then it turned out that the simple old gentleman, between his desire for notoriety and his eagerness to expose corruption, had been made the victim of a cruel joke. Some waggish colleagues had pointed out to him an itinerant Jew, who haunted the lobby and sold spectacles, as an agent of the fifth estate. From him the old gentleman had, after some clumsy angling and many leading questions, procured what he supposed to be an offer of money for his vote, which, by a ludicrous misunderstanding, managed by his humorous colleagues, was made to appear in his eyes as having received Mr. Frear's indorsement. Mr. Glenn's charges ended, therefore, in a ridiculous fiasco, and in a tremendous outburst of offended legislative virtue. The committee reported on the 10th; every one was exonerated; Mr. Glenn was brought to the bar and censured, and the next day he resigned. As for the astonished pedler, he was banished from the lobby, imprisoned, prosecuted, and forgotten. The display of indignation on the part of Mr. Glenn's brother legislators was, in view of the manifest absurdity of the whole affair, somewhat superfluous and somewhat suspicious; but one such false accusation protects a multitude of real sins. The trade of censor of morals fell into disrepute at Albany; and, under the shadow of this parody upon exposures of corruption, Mr. Gould was at liberty to devote himself to serious business without fear of interruption.

The full and true history of this legislative campaign will never be known. If the official reports of investigating committees are to be believed, Mr. Gould at about this time underwent a curious psychological metamorphosis, and suddenly became the veriest simpleton in money matters that ever fell into the hands of happy sharpers. Cunning lobby members had but to pretend to an influence over legislative minds, which every one knew they did not possess, to draw unlimited amounts from this verdant *habitué* of Wall Street. It seemed strange that he could have lived so long and learned so little. He dealt in large sums. He gave to one man, in whom he said "he did not take much stock," the sum of $5,000, "just to smooth him over." This man had just before received $5,000 of Erie money from another agent of the company. It would, therefore, be interesting to know what sums Mr. Gould paid to those individuals in whom he did "take much stock." Another individual is reported to have received $100,000 from one side, "to influence legislation," and to have subsequently received $70,000 from the other side to disappear with the money; which he accordingly did, and thereafter became a gentleman of elegant leisure. One senator was openly charged in the columns of the press with receiving a bribe of $20,000 from one side, and a second bribe of $15,000 from the other; but Mr. Gould's foggy mental condition only enabled him to be "perfectly astounded" at the action of this senator, though he knew nothing of any such transactions. Other senators were blessed with a sudden accession of wealth, but in no case was there any jot or tittle of proof of bribery. Mr. Gould's rooms at the Develin House overflowed with a joyous company, and his checks were numerous and heavy; but why he signed them, or what became of them, he seemed to know less than any man in Albany. This strange and expensive hallucination lasted until about the middle of April, when Mr. Gould was happily restored to his normal condition of a shrewd, acute, energetic man of business; nor is it known that he has since experienced any relapse into financial idiotcy.

About the period of Mr. Gould's arrival in Albany the tide turned, and soon began to flow strongly in favor of Erie and against Vanderbilt. How much of this was due to the skilful manipulations of Gould, and how much to the rising popular feeling against the practical consolidation of competing lines, cannot be decided. The popular protests did indeed pour in by scores, but then again the Erie secret-service money poured out like water. Yet Mr. Gould's task was sufficiently difficult. After the adverse report of the Senate committee, and the decisive defeat of the bill introduced into the Assembly, any favorable legislation seemed almost hopeless. Both Houses were committed. Vanderbilt had but to prevent action,—to keep things where they were, and the return of his opponents to New York was impracticable, unless with his consent; he appeared, in fact, to be absolute master of the situation. It seemed almost impossible to introduce a bill in the face of his great influence, and to navigate it through the many stages of legislative action and executive approval, without somewhere giving him an opportunity to defeat it. This was the task Gould had before him, and he accomplished it. On the 13th of April a bill, which met the approval of the Erie party, and which Judge Barnard subsequently compared not inaptly to a bill legalizing counterfeit money, was taken up in the Senate; for some days it was warmly debated, and on the 18th was passed by the decisive vote of seventeen to twelve. Senator Mattoon had not listened to the debate in vain. Perhaps his reason was convinced, or perhaps he had sold out new "points" and was again cheating himself or somebody else; at any rate, that thrifty senator was found voting with the majority. The bill practically legalized the recent issues of bonds, but made it a felony to use the proceeds of the sale of these bonds except for completing, furthering, and operating the road. The guaranty of the bonds of connecting roads was authorized, all contracts for consolidation or division of receipts between the Erie and the Vanderbilt roads were forbidden, and a clumsy provision was enacted that no stockholder, director, or officer in one of the Vanderbilt roads should be an officer or director in the Erie, and *vice versa*. The bill was, in fact, an amended copy of the one voted down so decisively in the Assembly a few days before, and it was in this body that the tug of war was expected to come.

The lobby was now full of animation; fabulous stories were told of the amounts which the contending parties were willing to expend; never before had the market quotations of votes and influence stood so high. The wealth of Vanderbilt seemed pitted against the Erie treasury, and the vultures flocked to Albany from every part of the State. Suddenly, at the very last moment, and even while special trains were bringing up fresh contestants to take part in the fray, a rumor ran through Albany as of some great public disaster, spreading panic and terror through hotel and corridor. The observer was reminded of the dark days of the war, when tidings came of some great defeat, as that on the Chickahominy or at Fredericksburg. In a moment the lobby was smitten with despair, and the cheeks of the legislators were blanched, for it was reported that Vanderbilt had withdrawn his opposition to the bill. The report was true. Either the Commodore had counted the cost and judged it excessive, or he despaired of the result. At any rate, he had yielded in advance. In a few moments the long struggle was over, and that bill which, in an unamended form, had but a few days before been thrown out of the Assembly by a vote of eighty-three to thirty-two, now passed it by a vote of one hundred and one to six, and was sent to the Governor for his signature. Then the wrath of the disappointed members turned on Vanderbilt. Decency was forgotten in a frenzied sense of disappointed avarice. That same night the *pro rata* freight bill, and a bill compelling the sale of through tickets by competing lines, were hurriedly passed, simply because they were thought hurtful to Vanderbilt; and the docket was ransacked in search of other measures, calculated to injure or annoy him. An adjournment, however, brought reflection, and subsequently, on this subject, the legislature stultified itself no more.

The bill had passed the legislature; would it receive the Executive signature? Here was the last stage of danger. For some time doubts were entertained on this point, and the last real conflict between the opposing interests took place in the Executive Chamber at Albany. There, on the afternoon of the 21st of April, Commodore Vanderbilt's counsel appeared before Governor Fenton, and urged upon him their reasons why the bill should be returned by him to the Senate without his signature. The arguments were patiently listened to, but, when they had closed, the Executive signature placed the seal of success upon Mr. Gould's labors at Albany. Even here the voice of calumny was not silent. As if this remarkable controversy was destined to leave a dark blot of suspicion upon every department of the civil service of New York, there were not wanting those who charged the Executive itself with the crowning act in this history of corruption. The very sum pretended to have been paid was named; the broker of Executive action was pointed out, and the number of minutes was specified which should intervene between the payment of the bribe and the signing of the law.[10]

Practically, the conflict was now over, and the period of negotiation had already begun. The combat in the courts was indeed kept up until far into May, for the angry passions of the lawyers and of the judges required time in which to wear themselves out. Day after day the columns of the press revealed fresh scandals to the astonished public, which at last grew indifferent to such revelations. Beneath all the wrangling of the courts, however, while the popular attention was distracted by the clatter of lawyers' tongues, the leaders in the controversy were quietly approaching a settlement. In the early days of his exile Mr. Drew had been more depressed in spirit, more vacillating in counsel, than his younger and more robust associates. The publicity and excitement which had sustained and even amused them had wearied and annoyed the old man. His mind had been oppressed with saucy doubts and tormented by officious advisers. Stronger wills than his were bearing him along with them; and though, perhaps, not more scrupulous than those about him, he was certainly less bold; their reckless daring shocked his more subtle and timid nature. He missed also his home comforts; he felt himself a prisoner in everything but in name; he knew that he was

[10] It is but justice to Governor Fenton to say, that, though this charge was boldly advanced by respectable journalists of his own party, it cannot be considered as sustained by the evidence. The testimony on the point will be found in the report of Senator Hale's investigating committee. Documents (Senate), 1869, No. 52, pp. 146–148, 151–155.

distrusted, and his every action watched by associates of whom he even stood in physical fear, who hardly allowed him to see his brokers alone, and did not respect the sanctity of his telegrams. After the first week or two, and as affairs began to assume a less untoward aspect, his spirits revived, and he soon began to make secret advances towards his angry opponent. The hostilities of the Stock Exchange are proverbially short-lived. A broker skilled in the ways of his kind gave it as his opinion, in one of these proceedings, that five minutes was the utmost period during which it was safe to count on the enmities or alliances of leading operators. Early in April Mr. Drew took advantage of that blessed immunity from arrest which the Sabbath confers on the hunted of the law, to revisit the familiar scenes across the river. His visit soon resulted in conferences between himself and Vanderbilt, and these conferences naturally led to overtures of peace. Though the tide was turning against the great railroad king, though an uncontrollable popular feeling was fast bearing down his schemes of monopoly, yet he was by no means beaten or subdued. His plans, however, had evidently failed for the present; as he expressed himself, he could easily enough buy up the Erie Railway, but he could not buy up the printing-press. It was now clearly his interest to abandon his late line of attack, and to bide his time patiently, or to possess himself of his prey by some other method. The wishes of all parties, therefore, were fixed on a settlement, and no one was disposed to stand out except in order to obtain better terms. The interests, however, were multifarious. There were four parties to be taken care of, and the depleted treasury of the Erie Railway was doomed to suffer.

The details of this masterpiece of Wall Street diplomacy have never come to light, but Mr. Drew's visits to New York became more frequent and less guarded; by the middle of April he had appeared in Broad Street on a week-day, undisturbed by fears of arrest, and soon rumors began to spread of misunderstandings between himself and his brother exiles. It was said that his continual absences alarmed them, that they distrusted him, that his terms of settlement were not theirs. It was even asserted that his orders on the treasury were no longer honored, and that he had, in fact, ceased to be a power in Erie. Whatever truth there may have been in these rumors, it was very evident his associates had no inclination to trust themselves within the reach of the New York courts until a definitive treaty, satisfactory to themselves, was signed and sealed. This probably took place about the 25th of April; for on that day the Erie camp at "Fort Taylor," as their uninviting hotel had been dubbed, was broken up, the President and one of the Executive Committee took steamer for Boston, and the other directors appeared before Judge Barnard, prepared to purge themselves of their contempt.

Though the details of negotiation have never been divulged, yet it was clear enough what three of the four parties desired. Commodore Vanderbilt wished to be relieved of the vast amount of stock with which he was loaded, and his friends Work and Schell, in whose names the battle had been fought, must be protected. Mr. Drew desired to settle his entangled accounts as treasurer, and to obtain a release in full, which might be pleaded in future complications. Mr. Eldridge and his Boston friends were sufficiently anxious to be relieved of the elephant they found on their hands, in the Erie Railway of New York, and to be at leisure to devote the spoils of their victim to the development of their New England enterprise. Messrs. Gould and Fisk alone were unprovided for, and they alone presented themselves as obstacles to be overcome by railroad diplomacy.

At last, upon the 2d of July, Mr. Eldridge formally announced to the Board of Directors that the terms of peace had been agreed upon. Commodore Vanderbilt was, in the first place, provided for. He was to be relieved of fifty thousand shares of Erie stock at 70, receiving therefor $2,500,000 in cash, and $1,250,000 in bonds of the Boston, Hartford, & Erie at 80. He was also to receive a further sum of $1,000,000 outright, as a consideration for the privilege the Erie road thus purchased of calling upon him for his remaining fifty thousand shares at 70 at any time within four months. He was also to have two seats in the Board of Directors, and all suits were to be dismissed and offences condoned. The sum of $429,250 was fixed upon as a proper amount to assuage the sense of wrong from which his two friends Work and Schell had suffered, and to efface from their memories all recollection of the unfortunate "pool" of the previous December. Why the owners of the Erie Railway should have paid this indemnity of $4,000,000 is not very clear. The operations were apparently outside of the business of a railway company, and no more connected with the stockholders of the Erie than were the butchers' bills of the individual directors.

While Vanderbilt and his friends were thus provided for, Mr. Drew was to be left in undisturbed enjoyment of the fruits of his recent operations, but was to pay into the treasury $540,000 and interest, in full discharge of all claims and causes of action which the Erie Company might have against him. The Boston party, as represented by Mr. Eldridge, was to be relieved of $5,000,000 of their Boston, Hartford, & Erie bonds, for which they were to receive $4,000,000 of Erie acceptances. None of these parties, therefore, had anything to complain of, whatever might be the sensations of the real owners of the railway. A total amount of some $9,000,000 in cash was drawn from the treasury in fulfilment of this *settlement,* as the persons concerned were pleased to term this remarkable disposition of property intrusted to their care.

Messrs. Gould and Fisk still remained to be taken care of, and to them their associates left—the Erie Railway. These gentlemen subsequently maintained that they had vehemently opposed this settlement, and had denounced it in the secret councils as a fraud and a robbery. Mr. Fisk was peculiarly outspoken in relation to it, and declared himself "thunderstruck and dumbfounded" that his brother directors whom he had supposed respectable men should have had anything to do with any such proceeding. A small portion of this statement is not wholly improbable. The astonishment at the turpitude of his fellow-officials was a little unnecessary in one who had already seen "more robbery" during the year of his connection with the Erie Railway than he had "ever seen before in the same space of time,"—so much of it indeed that he dated his "gray hairs" from that 7th of October which saw his election to the board. That Mr. Fisk and Mr. Gould were extremely indignant at a partition of plunder from which they were excluded is, however, very certain. The rind of the orange is not generally considered the richest part of the fruit; a corporation on the verge of bankruptcy is less coveted, even by operators in Wall Street, than one rich in valuable assets. Probably at this time these gentlemen seriously debated the expediency of resorting again to a war of injunctions, and carefully kept open a way for doing so; however this may have been, they seem finally to have concluded that there was yet plunder left in the poor old hulk, and so, after four stormy interviews, all opposition was at last withdrawn and the definitive treaty was finally signed.[11] Mr. Eldridge thereupon counted out his bonds and received his acceptances, which latter were cashed at once to close up the transaction, and at once he resigned his position as director and president. The

[11] The account given of this affair by Mr. Fisk from the witness stand on a subsequent occasion was characteristic: "Finally about twelve o'clock a paper was passed round and we signed it; I don't know what it contained; I didn't read it; I don't think I noticed a word of it; I remember the space for the names was greater than that covered by the writing; my impression is that I took my hat and left at once in disgust; I told Gould we had sold ourselves to the Devil; I presume that was not the only document signed; I remember seeing Mr. White, the cashier, come in with the check-book, and I said to him, 'You are bearing in the remains of this corporation to be put in Vanderbilt's tomb.' No; I didn't know the contents of the paper which I signed, and I have always been glad that I didn't; I have thought of it a thousand times; I don't know what other documents I signed; I signed everything that was put before me; after once the Devil had hold of me I kept on signing; didn't read any of them and have no idea what they were; I don't know how many I signed; I kept no count after the first one; I went with the robbers then and I have been with them ever since; my impression is that after the signing I left at once; I don't know whether we sat down or not; we didn't have anything to eat, I know."

Boston raiders then retired, heavy with spoil, into their own North country, and there proceeded to build up an Erie influence for New England, in which task they labored with assiduity and success. Gradually they here introduced the more highly developed civilization of the land of their temporary adoption and boldly attempted to make good their private losses from the public treasury. A more barefaced scheme of plunder never was devised, and yet the executive veto alone stood between it and success. These, however, were the events of another year and unconnected with this narrative, from which these characters in the Erie management henceforth disappear. For the rest it is only necessary to say that Mr. Vanderbilt, relieved of his heavy load of its stock, apparently ceased to concern himself with Erie; while Daniel Drew, released from the anxieties of office, assumed for a space the novel character of a looker-on in Wall Street.

III

Thus, in the early days of July, Messrs. Fisk and Gould found themselves beginning life, as it were, in absolute control of the Erie Railway, but with an empty treasury and a doubtful reputation. Outwardly things did not look unpromising. The legal complications were settled, and the fearful load imposed by the settlement upon the already overburdened resources of the road was not, of course, imparted to the public. It is unnecessary to add that the "outside" holders of the stock were, in the counsels of the managers, included in that public the inquiries of which in regard to the affairs of the company were looked upon by the ring in control as downright impertinence. A calm—deceitful indeed, but yet a calm—succeeded the severe agitations of the money market. All through the month of July money was easy and ruled at three or four per cent; Erie was consequently high, and was quoted at about seventy, which enabled the company to dispose without loss of the Vanderbilt stock. It may well be believed that Messrs. Fisk and Gould could not have regarded their empty treasury, just depleted to the extent of nine millions,—trust funds misapplied by directors in the processes of stock-gambling,—without serious question as to their ability to save the road from bankruptcy. The October election was approaching, Vanderbilt was still a threatening element in the future, and new combinations might arise. Millions were necessary, and must at once be forthcoming. The new officials were, however, men of resource, and were not men of many scruples. The money must be raised, and recent experience indicated a method of raising it. Their policy, freed from the influence of Drew's vacillating, treacherous, and withal timid nature, could now be bold and direct. The pretence of resistance to monopoly would always serve them, as it had served them before, as a plausible and popular cry. Above all, their councils were now free from interlopers and spies; for the first act of Messrs. Gould and Fisk had been to do away with the old board of auditors, and to concentrate all power in their own hands as president, treasurer, and controller. Fortunately for them it was midsummer, and the receipts of the road were very heavy, supplying them with large sums of ready money; [12] most fortunately for them, also,

[12] It will be remembered that the act of 21st April, legalizing the issue of bonds, made it a felony to devote the proceeds to any purpose except equipping, constructing, and operating the road. Mr. Gould's explanation of the effect he gave to this clause is not only amusing as a piece of impudence, but extremely suggestive as regards the efficacy of legislation. Mr. Gould, be it remembered, procured the passage of the law, and Mr. Gould thus explains to the railroad committee of the legislature the force he gave to its provisions.

Mr. Gould. . . . . The law is, that you can only use the money realized on these bonds for the purpose of equipping, constructing, and operating the road, and therefore I had to use the earnings of the road to meet these large liabilities, which had been authorized by the board (the Eldridge-Vanderbilt settlement), and use the money realized from the bonds to equip, construct, and operate the road. . . . .

Question by Mr. Waterman. In fact these twenty million of bonds were issued to meet these obligations, and not for the purpose of maintaining, operating, and constructing the road?

a strange infatuation at this time took possession of the English mind.

Shrewd as the British capitalist proverbially is, his judgment in regard to American investments has been singularly fallible. When our national bonds went begging at a discount of sixty per cent, he transmitted them to Germany and refused to touch them himself. At the very same time a class of railroad securities—such as those of this very Erie Railway, or, to cite a yet stronger case, those of the Atlantic & Great Western road—was gradually absorbed in London as an honest investment long after these securities had "gone into the street" in America. It was this strange fatuity which did much to bring on the crash of May, 1866. Even that did not seem to teach wisdom to the British bankers, who had apparently passed from the extreme of caution to the extreme of confidence. They now, after all the exposures of the preceding months, rushed into Erie, apparently because it seemed cheap, and the prices in New York were sustained by the steady demand for stock on foreign account. Not only did this curious infatuation, involving purchases to the extent of a hundred thousand shares, cover up the operations of the new ring, but, at a later period, the date of the possible return of this stock to Wall Street was the hinge on which the success of its culminating plot was made to turn.

The appearance of calm lasted but about thirty days. Early in August it was evident that something was going on. Erie suddenly fell ten per cent; in a few days more it experienced

---

Answer. No, sir; I used the earnings of the road to meet these obligations. . . . . We had to live up to the letter of the law, and use the money realized from the bonds for the purpose of operating, constructing, and equipping the road.

Q. But your pressing need of money was not for the purpose of operating the road, but for the purpose of meeting these obligations.

A. Yes, sir.

Q. The amount of money you sought to raise was the amount of these obligations?

A. Yes, sir.

a further fall of seven per cent, touching 44 by the 19th of the month, upon which day, to the astonishment of Wall Street, the transfer-books of the company were closed preparatory to the annual election. As this election was not to take place until the 13th of October, and as the books had thus been closed thirty days in advance of the usual time, it looked very much as though the managers were satisfied with the present disposition of the stock, and meant, by keeping it where it was, to preclude any such unpleasantness as an opposition ticket. The courts and a renewed war of injunctions were of course open to any contestants, including Commodore Vanderbilt, who might desire to avail themselves of them; probably, however, the memory of recent struggles was too fresh to permit any one to embark on those treacherous waters. At any rate, nothing of the sort was attempted. The election took place at the usual time, and the ring in control voted itself, without opposition, into a new lease of power. Two new names had meanwhile appeared in the list of Erie directors,—those of Peter B. Sweeney and William M. Tweed, the two most prominent leaders of that notorious ring which controls the proletariat of New York City and governs the politics of the State. The alliance was an ominous one, for the construction of the new board can be stated in few words, and calls for no comment. It consisted of the Erie ring and the Tammany ring, brought together in close political and financial union; and, for the rest, a working majority of supple tools and a hopeless minority of respectable figure-heads. This formidable combination shot out its feelers far and wide: it wielded the influence of a great corporation with a capital of a hundred millions; it controlled the politics of the first city of the New World; it sent its representatives to the Senate of the State, and numbered among its agents the judges of the courts. Compact, disciplined, and reckless, it knew its own power and would not scruple to use it.

It was now the month of October, and the harvest had been gathered. The ring and its allies determined to reap their harvest also, and that harvest was to be nothing less than a contribution levied, not only upon Wall Street and New York, but upon all the immense interests, commercial and financial, which radiate from New York all over the country. Like the Cæsar of old, they issued their edict that all the world should be taxed. The process was not novel, but it was effective. A monetary stringency may be looked for in New York at certain seasons of every year. It is generally most severe in the autumn months, when the crops have to be moved, and the currency is drained steadily away from the financial centre towards the extremities of the system. The method by which an artificial stringency is produced is thus explained in a recent report of the Comptroller of the Currency: "It is scarcely possible to avoid the inference that nearly one half of the available resources of the national banks in the city of New York are used in the operations of the stock and gold exchange; that they are loaned upon the security of stocks which are bought and sold largely on speculation, and which are manipulated by cliques and combinations, according as the bulls or bears are for the moment in the ascendency. . . . . Taking advantage of an active demand for money to move the crops West and South, shrewd operators form their combination to depress the market by 'locking up' money,—withdrawing all they can control or borrow from the common fund; money becomes scarce, the rate of interest advances, and stocks decline. The legitimate demand for money continues; and, fearful of trenching on their reserve, the banks are strained for means. They dare not call in their demand loans, for that would compel their customers to sell securities on a falling market, which would make matters worse. Habitually lending their means to the utmost limit of prudence, and their credit much beyond that limit, to brokers and speculators, they are powerless to afford relief;—their customers by the force of circumstances become their masters. The banks cannot hold back or withdraw from the dilemma in which their mode of doing business has placed them. They must carry the load to save their margins. A panic which should greatly reduce the price of securities would occasion serious, if not fatal, results to the banks most extensively engaged in such operations, and would produce a feeling of insecurity which would be very dangerous to the entire banking interest of the country." [13]

All this machinery was now put in motion; the banks and their customers were forced into the false position described, and towards the end of October it had become perfectly notorious in Wall Street that large new issues of Erie had been made, and that these new issues were intimately connected with the sharp stringency then existing in the money market. It was at last determined to investigate the matter, and upon the 27th of the month a committee of three was appointed by the Stock Exchange to wait upon the officers of the corporation with the view of procuring such information as they might be willing to impart. The committee called on Mr. Gould and stated the object of their visit. In reply to their inquiries Mr. Gould informed them that Erie convertible bonds for ten millions of dollars had been issued, half of which had already been, and the rest of which would be, converted into stock; that the money had been devoted to the purchase of Boston, Hartford, & Erie bonds for five millions, and also—of course—to payments for steel rails. The committee desired to know if any further issue of stock was in contemplation, but were obliged to rest satisfied with a calm assurance that no new issue was just then contemplated except "in certain contingencies"; from which enigmatical utterances Wall Street was left to infer that the exigencies of Messrs. Gould and Fisk were elements not to be omitted from any calculations as to the future of Erie and the money market. The amount of these issues of new stock was, of course, soon whispered in a general way; but it was not till months afterwards that a sworn statement of the secretary of the Erie Railway revealed the fact that the stock of the corporation had been increased from $34,265,300 on the 1st of July, 1868, the date when Drew and his associates had left it, to $57,766,300 on the 24th of October of the same year, or by two hundred

13 Finance Report, 1868, pp. 20, 21.

and thirty-five thousand shares in four months.[14] This, too, had been done without consultation with the board of directors, and with no other authority than that conferred by the ambiguous resolution of February 19. Under that resolution the stock of the company had now been increased one hundred and thirty-eight per cent in eight months. Such a process of inflation may, perhaps, be justly considered the most extraordinary feat of financial legerdemain which history has yet recorded.

Now, however, when the committee of the Stock Exchange had returned to those who sent them, the mask was thrown off, and operations were conducted with vigor and determination. New issues of Erie were continually forced upon the market until the stock fell to 35; greenbacks were locked up in the vaults of the banks, until the unexampled sum of twelve millions was withdrawn from circulation; the prices of securities and merchandise declined; trade and the autumnal movement of the crops were brought almost to a stand-still; and loans became more and more difficult to negotiate, until at length even one and a half per cent a day was paid for carrying stocks. Behind all this it was notorious that some one was pulling the wires, the slightest touch upon which sent a quiver through every nerve of the great financial organism, and wrung private gain from public agony. The strange proceeding reminds one of those scenes in the chambers of the Inquisition where the judges calmly put their victim to the question, until his spasms warned them not to exceed the limits of human endurance. At last the public distress reached the ears of the government at Washington. While it was simply the gamblers of Wall Street who were

[14] In April, 1871, although the stock was then nominally registered, a further secret issue was made by which some $600,000 in cash was realized on $3,000,000 of stock. Periodical issues had then carried the gross amount up to the neighborhood of $86,500,000; or from a total of 250,000 shares, when the management changed at the election of October 17, 1867, to 865,000 shares within four years. Apparently Mr. Fisk was more correct than usual in his statement, when he remarked, that, having once joined the robbers, "he had been with them ever since."

tearing each other, their clamor for relief excited little sympathy. When, however, the suffering had extended through all the legitimate business circles of the country,—when the scarcity of money threatened to cut off the winter food of the poor, to rob the farmer of the fruits of his toil, and to bring ruin upon half the debtor class of the community,—then even Mr. McCulloch, pledged as he was to contraction, was moved to interfere. The very revenues of the government were affected by the operations of gamblers. They were therefore informed that, if necessary, fifty millions of additional currency would be forthcoming to the relief of the community, and then, and not till then, the screws were loosened.

The harvest of the speculators, however, was still but half gathered. Hitherto the combination had operated for a fall. Now was the moment to change the tactics and take advantage of the rise. The time was calculated to a nicety. The London infatuation had wonderfully continued, and as fast as certificates of stock were issued they seemed to take wings across the Atlantic. Yet there was a limit even to English credulity, and in November it became evident that the agents of foreign houses were selling their stock to arrive. The price was about 40; the certificates might be expected by the steamer of the 23d. Instantly the combination changed front. As before they had depressed the market, they now ran it up, and, almost as if by magic, the stock, which had been heavy at 40, astonished every one by shooting up to 50. New developments were evidently at hand.

At this point Mr. Daniel Drew once more made his appearance on the stage. As was very natural, he had soon wearied of the sameness of his part as a mere looker-on in Wall Street, and had relapsed into his old habits. He was no longer treasurer of the Erie, and could not therefore invite the public to the game, while he himself with sombre piety shook the loaded dice. But it had become with him a second nature to operate in Erie, and once more he was deep in its movements. At first he had combined with his old friends, the present directors, in their "locking-up" conspiracy. He had agreed to assist them to the extent of four millions. The vacillating, timid nature of the man, however, could not keep pace with his more daring and determined associates, and, after embarking a million, becoming alarmed at the success of the joint operations and the remonstrances of those who were threatened with ruin, he withdrew his funds from the operators' control and himself from their councils. But though he did not care to run the risk or to incur the odium, he had no sort of objection to sharing the spoils. Knowing, therefore, or supposing that he knew, the plan of campaign, and that plan jumping with his own bearish inclinations, he continued, on his own account, operations looking to a fall. One may easily conceive the wrath of the Erie operators at such a treacherous policy; and it is not difficult to imagine their vows of vengeance. Meanwhile all went well with Daniel Drew. Erie looked worse and worse, and the golden harvest seemed drawing near. By the middle of November he had contracted for the delivery of some seventy thousand shares at current prices, averaging, perhaps, 38, and probably was counting his gains. He did not appreciate the full power and resources of his old associates. On the 14th of November their tactics changed, and he found himself involved in terrible entanglements,—hopelessly cornered. His position disclosed itself on Saturday. Naturally the first impulse was to have recourse to the courts. An injunction—a dozen injunctions—could be had for the asking, but, unfortunately, could be had by both parties. Drew's own recent experience, and his intimate acquaintance with the characters of Fisk and Gould, were not calculated to inspire him with much confidence in the efficacy of the law. But nothing else remained, and, after hurried consultations among the victims, the lawyers were applied to, the affidavits were prepared, and it was decided to repair on the following Monday to the so-called courts of justice.

Nature, however, had not bestowed on Daniel Drew the steady nerve and sturdy gambler's pride of either Vanderbilt or of his old companions at Jersey City. His mind wavered and hesitated between different courses of action. His only care was for himself, his only thought was of his own position. He was willing to betray one party or the other, as the case might be. He had given his affidavit to those who were to bring the suit on the Monday, but he stood perfectly ready to employ Sunday in betraying their counsels to the defendants in the suit. A position more contemptible, a state of mind more pitiable, can hardly be conceived. After passing the night in this abject condition, on the morning of Sunday he sought out Mr. Fisk for purposes of self-humiliation and treachery.[15] He then partially revealed the difficulties of his situation, only to have his confidant prove to him how entirely he was caught, by completing to him the revelation. He betayed the secrets of his new allies, and bemoaned his own hard fate; he was thereupon comforted by Mr. Fisk with the cheery remark that "he (Drew) was the last man who ought to whine over any position in which he placed himself in regard to Erie." The poor man begged to see Mr. Gould, and would take no denial. Finally Mr. Gould was brought in, and the scene was repeated for his edification. The two must have been satiated with revenge. At last they sent him away, promising to see him again that evening. At the hour named he again appeared, and, after waiting their convenience,—for they spared him no humiliation,—he again appealed to them, offering them great sums if they would issue new stock or lend him of their stock. He implored, he argued, he threatened. At the end of two hours of humiliation, persuaded that it was all in vain, that he was wholly in the power of antagonists without mercy, he took his hat, said, "I will bid you good night," and went his way.

There is a touch of nature about this scene which reads like fiction. Indeed, it irresistibly recalls the feebler effort of Dickens to portray Fagin's last night alive, and there is more pathos in the parting address than in the Jew's,—"An old man, my lord! a very, very old man." But the truth is stranger

15 It ought perhaps to be stated that this portion of the narrative has no stronger foundation than an affidavit of Mr. Fisk, which has not, however, been publicly contradicted.

than fiction. Dickens did not dare picture the old "fence" in Oliver Twist turned out of his own house and stripped of his plunder by the very hands through which he had procured it. In the case of Daniel Drew, however, the ideal poetic justice was brought about in fact; the evil instructions returned to plague the inventor, and it is hard to believe that, as he left the Erie offices that night, his apt pupils, even as those of Fagin might have done, did not watch his retiring steps with suppressed merriment; and, when the door had closed upon him, that the one did not explode in loud bursts of laughter, while the other, with a quiet chuckle, plunged his hands into those capacious pockets which yawned for all the wealth of Erie. Bad as all these things are, terrible as is the condition of affairs only partially revealed, there is a grim humor running through them which ever makes itself felt.

But to return to the course of events. With the lords of Erie forewarned was forearmed. They knew something of the method of procedure in New York courts of law. At this particular juncture Mr. Justice Sutherland, a magistrate of such pure character and unsullied reputation that it is inexplicable how he ever came to be elevated to the bench on which he sits, was holding chambers, according to assignment, for the four weeks between the first Monday in November and the first Monday in December. By a rule of the court, all applications for orders during that time were to be made before him, and he only, according to the courtesy of the Bench, took cognizance of such proceedings. Some general arrangement of this nature is manifestly necessary to avoid continual conflicts of jurisdiction. The details of the assault on the Erie directors having been settled, counsel appeared before Judge Sutherland on Monday morning, and petitioned for an injunction restraining the Erie directors from any new issue of stock or the removal of the funds of the company beyond the jurisdiction of the court, and also asking that the road be placed in the hands of a receiver. The suit was brought in the name of Mr. August Belmont, who was supposed to represent large foreign holders. The petition set forth at length the alleged facts in the case, and was supported by the affidavits of Mr. Drew and others. Mr. Drew apparently did not inform the counsel of the manner in which he had passed his leisure hours on the previous day; had he done so, Mr. Belmont's counsel probably would have expedited their movements. The injunction was, however, duly signed, and, doubtless, immediately served.

Meanwhile Messrs. Gould and Fisk had not been idle. Applications for injunctions and receiverships were a game which two could play at, and long experience had taught these close observers the very great value of the initiative in law. Accordingly, some two hours before the Belmont application was made, they had sought no less a person than Mr. Justice Barnard, caught him, as it were, either in his bed or at his breakfast, whereupon he had held a *lit de justice,* and made divers astonishing orders. A petition was presented in the name of one McIntosh, a salaried officer of the Erie Road, who claimed also to be a shareholder. It set forth the danger of injunctions and of the appointment of a receiver, the great injury likely to result therefrom, etc. After due consideration on the part of Judge Barnard, an injunction was issued, staying and restraining all suits, and actually appointing Jay Gould receiver, to hold and disburse the funds of the company in accordance with the resolutions of the Board of Directors and the Executive Committee. This certainly was a very brilliant flank movement, and testified not less emphatically to Gould's genius than to Barnard's law; but most of all did it testify to the efficacy of the new combination between Tammany Hall and the Erie Railway. Since the passage of the bill "to legalize counterfeit money," in April, and the present November, new light had burst upon the judicial mind, and as the news of one injunction and a vague rumor of the other crept through Wall Street that day, it was no wonder that operators stood aghast and that Erie fluctuated wildly from 50 to 61 and back to 48.

The Erie directors, however, did not rest satisfied with the position which they had won through Judge Barnard's order.

That simply placed them, as it were, in a strong defensive attitude. They were not the men to stop there: they aspired to nothing less than a vigorous offensive. With a superb audacity, which excites admiration, the new trustee immediately filed a supplementary petition. Therein it was duly set forth that doubts had been raised as to the legality of the recent issue of some two hundred thousand shares of stock, and that only about this amount was to be had in America; the trustee therefore petitioned for authority to use the funds of the corporation to purchase and cancel the whole of this amount at any price less than the par value, without regard to the rate at which it had been issued. The desired authority was conferred by Mr. Justice Barnard as soon as asked. Human assurance could go no further. The petitioners had issued these shares in the bear interest at 40, and had run down the value of Erie to 35; they had then turned round, and were now empowered to buy back that very stock in the bull interest, and in the name and with the funds of the corporation, at par. A law of the State distinctly forbade corporations from operating in their own stock; but this law was disregarded as if it had been only an injunction. An injunction forbade the treasurer from making any disposition of the funds of the company, and this injunction was respected no more than the law. These trustees had sold the property of their wards at 40; they were now prepared to use the money of their wards to buy the same property back at 80, and a judge had been found ready to confer on them the power to do so. Drew could not withstand such tactics, and indeed the annals of Wall Street furnished no precedent or parallel. They might have furnished one, but the opportunity had been lost. Had Robert Schuyler not lived fifteen years too soon,—had he, instead of flying his country and dying broken-hearted in exile, boldly attempted a change of front when his fraudulent issues had filled Wall Street with panic, and had he sought to use the funds of his company for a masterly upward movement in his own manufactured stock,—then, though in those uncultivated and illiberal days his scheme might have come to naught, and he himself might even have passed from the presence of an indignant jury into the keeping of a surly jailer, at least he would have evinced a mind in advance of his day, and could have comforted himself with the assurance that he was the first of a line of great men, and that the time was not far distant when his name and his fame would be cherished among the most brilliant recollections of Wall Street. But Schuyler lived before his time!

When this last, undreamed-of act was made public on Wednesday at noon, it was apparent that the crisis was not far off. Daniel Drew was cornered. Erie was scarce and selling at 47, and would not become plenty until the arrival of the English steamer on Monday; and so, at 47, Mr. Drew flung himself into the breach to save his endangered credit, and, under his purchases, the stock rapidly rose, until at five o'clock Wednesday afternoon it reached 57. Contrary to expectation, the "corner" had not yet culminated. It became evident the next morning that before two o'clock that day the issue would be decided. Drew fought desperately. The Brokers' Board was wild with excitement. High words passed; collisions took place; the bears were savage, and the bulls pitiless. Erie touched 62, and there was a difference of sixteen per cent between cash stock and stock sold to be delivered in three days,—when the steamer would be in,—and a difference of ten per cent between stock to be delivered on the spot and that to be delivered at the usual time, which was a quarter after two o'clock. Millions were handled like thousands; fabulous rates of interest were paid; rumors of legal proceedings were flying about, and forays of the Erie chiefs on the Vanderbilt roads were confidently predicted. New York Central suddenly shot up seven per cent under these influences, and Vanderbilt seemed about to enter the field. The interest of the stock market centred in the combatants and on these two great corporations. All other stocks were quiet and neglected while the giants were fighting it out. The battle was too fierce to last long. At a quarter before three o'clock the struggle would be over. Yet now, at the very last moment, the prize which trembled before them eluded the grasp of the Erie ring. Their opponent was not saved, but they shared his disaster. Their combination had turned on the fact, disclosed to them by the Erie books, that some three hundred thousand shares of its stock had been issued in the ten-share certificates which alone are transmitted to London. This amount they supposed to be out of the country; the balance they could account for as beyond the reach of Drew. Suddenly, as two o'clock approached, and Erie was trembling in the sixties, all Broadway—every tailor and boot-maker and cigar-vender of New York—seemed pouring into Broad Street, and each new-comer held eagerly before him one or more of those ten-share certificates which should have been in London. Not only this, but the pockets of the agents of foreign bankers seemed bursting with them. Bedlam had suddenly broken loose in Wall Street. It was absolutely necessary for the conspirators to absorb this stock, to keep it from the hands of Drew. This they attempted to do, and manfully stood their ground, fighting against time. Suddenly, when the hour had almost come,—when five minutes more would have landed them in safety,—through one of those strange incidents which occur in Wall Street and which cannot be explained, they seemed smitten with panic. It is said their bank refused to certify their checks for the suddenly increased amount; the sellers insisted on having certified checks, and, in the delay caused by this unforeseen difficulty, the precious five minutes elapsed, and the crisis had passed. The fruits of their plot had escaped them. Drew made good his contracts at 57, the stock at once fell heavily to 42, and a dull quiet succeeded to the excitement of the morning. The hand of the government had made itself felt in Wall Street.

The Broad Street conflict was over, and some one had reaped a harvest. Who was it? It was not Drew, for his losses, apart from a ruined prestige, were estimated at nearly a million and a half of dollars. The Erie directors were not the fortunate men, for their only trophies were great piles of certificates of Erie stock, which had cost them "corner" prices, and for which no demand existed. If Drew's loss was a million and a half, their loss was likely to be nearer three millions. Who, then, were the recipients of these missing millions? There is an ancient saying, which seems to have been tolerably verified in this case, that when certain persons fall out certain other persons come by their dues. The "corner" was very beautiful in all its details, and most admirably planned; but, unfortunately, those who engineered it had just previously made the volume of stock too large for accurate calculation. For once the outside public had been at hand and Wall Street had been found wanting. A large portion of the vast sum taken from the combatants found its way into the pockets of the agents of English bankers, and a part of it was accounted for by them to their principals; another portion went to relieve anxious holders among the American outside public; the remainder fell to professional operators, probably far more lucky than sagacious. Still, there had been a fall before there was a rise. The subsequent disaster, perhaps, no more than counterbalanced the earlier victory; at any rate, Messrs. Gould and Fisk did not succumb, but preserved a steady front, and Erie was more upon the street than ever. In fact, it was wholly there now. The recent operations had proved too outrageous even for the Brokers' Board. A new rule was passed, that no stock should be called, the issues of which were not registered at some respectable banking-house. The Erie directors declined to conform to this rule, and their road was stricken from the list of calls. Nothing daunted at this, these Protean creatures at once organized a new board of their own, and so far succeeded in their efforts as to have Erie quoted and bought and sold as regularly as ever.

Though the catastrophe had taken place on the 19th, the struggle was not yet over. The interests involved were so enormous, the developments so astounding, such passions had been aroused, that some safety-valve through which suppressed wrath could work itself off was absolutely necessary, and this the courts of law afforded. The attack was stimulated by various motives. The *bona fide* holders of the stock, especially the foreign holders, were alarmed for the existence of their property. The Erie ring had now boldly taken the position that their duty was, not to manage the road in the interests of its owners, not to make it a dividend-paying corporation, but to preserve it from consolidation with the Vanderbilt monopoly. This policy was openly proclaimed by Mr. Gould, at a later day, before an investigating committee at Albany. With unspeakable effrontery,—an effrontery so great as actually to impose on his audience and a portion of the press, and make them believe that the public ought to wish him success,—he described how stock issues at the proper time, to any required amount, could alone keep him in control of the road, and keep Mr. Vanderbilt out of it; it would be his duty, therefore, he argued, to issue as much new stock, at about the time of the annual election, as would suffice to keep a majority of all the stock in existence under his control; and he declared that he meant to do this.[16] The strangest thing of all was, that it never seemed to occur to his audience that the propounder of this comical sophistry was a trustee and

[16] *Question to Mr. Gould.* For the information of the committee, would you give us your opinion as to the utility of that section of the general railroad law, under which so many issues of convertible bonds have been made?

Answer. I could only speak as to the Erie Road; that law saved the Erie Road from bankruptcy; and as long as that law is unrepealed, I should do what I did again. I should save the road. I think it is a good law.

Q. Is it not liable to abuse?

A. I have never known it to be abused; if that was repealed, I think that Mr. Vanderbilt would have the road; but as long as it is not repealed it is held *in terrorem* over him.

Q. Suppose the section was amended so as to require the consent of the stockholders?

A. Suppose he owned all the stock, what would be the difference? . . . .

Q. What other effect would it (the repeal of Section 10) have?

A. I think it would lay the State open to a great monopoly,—the greatest the world has ever seen.

Much more followed in the same style. One remark of Mr. Gould's, however, in this examination, bore the stamp of truth and perspicuity. It is recorded as follows: "The Erie road won't be a dividend-paying road for a long time on its common stock."

guardian for the stockholders, and not a public benefactor; and that the owners of the Erie Road might possibly prefer not to be deprived of their property, in order to secure the blessing of competition. So unique a method of securing a re-election was probably never before suggested with a grave face, and yet, if we may believe the reporters, Mr. Gould, in developing it, produced a very favorable impression on the committee. It was hardly to be expected that such advanced views as to the duties and powers of railway directors would favorably impress commonplace individuals who might not care to have their property scaled down to meet Mr. Gould's views of public welfare. These persons accordingly, popularly supposed to be represented by Mr. Belmont, wished to get their property out of the hands of such fanatics in the cause of cheap transportation and plentiful stock, with the least possible delay. Combined with these were the operators who had suffered in the late "corner," and who desired to fight for better terms and a more equal division of plunder. Behind them all, Vanderbilt was supposed to be keeping an eager eye on the long-coveted Erie. Thus the materials for litigation existed in abundance.

On Monday, the 23d, Judge Sutherland vacated Judge Barnard's order appointing Jay Gould receiver, and, after seven hours' argument and some exhibitions of vulgarity and indecency on the part of counsel, which vied with those of the previous April, he appointed Mr. Davies, an ex-chief justice of the Court of Appeals, receiver of the road and its franchise, leaving the special terms of the order to be settled at a future day. The seven hours' struggle had not been without an object; that day Judge Barnard had been peculiarly active. The morning hours he had beguiled by the delivery to the grand jury of one of the most astounding charges ever recorded; and now, as the shades of evening were falling, he closed the labors of the day by issuing a stay of the proceedings then pending before his associate.[17] Tuesday had

[17] The charge referred to is altogether too curious to be forgotten; it was couched in the following terms:—

been named by Judge Sutherland, at the time he appointed his receiver, as the day upon which he would settle the details of the order. His first proceeding upon that day, on finding his action stayed by Judge Barnard, was to grant a motion to show cause, on the next day, why Barnard's order should not be vacated. This style of warfare, however, savored altogether too much of the tame defensive to meet successfully the bold strategy of Messrs. Gould and Fisk. They carried the war into Africa. In the twenty-four hours during which Judge Sutherland's order to show cause was pending three

---

"GENTLEMEN OF THE GRAND JURY,—I deem it not inappropriate at the present time to call your attention to three or four subjects that, in my judgment, the grand jury should look into: First, in regard to alleged frauds at elections; second, in regard to the alleged corruptions of the judiciary here; third, as to the action of certain newspapers in New York in perpetrating daily and hourly libels. I had intended, gentlemen, at the commencement of this term, to have gone over many of these subjects more fully than I can now; but I am led to-day not to delay it any longer in consequence of the annoyance I am subjected to by newspapers and letterwriters, not borne out, of all sorts of vilifications and abuses for offences of which I certainly know nothing, and see if the writers of some of these articles cannot be made to come before you and substantiate some among the many of the different allegations that they have made against the judge that now addresses you. In to-day's Tribune and to-day's Times, along with articles in the Jersey papers and elsewhere, are charges of the most atrocious character made against corruptions, in interfering with the duties of electors, and charging the judge with being in a combination in Wall Street. Now, it is unnecessary for me to say to you that he never bought or sold or owned a share of stock in his life, and as for the large fortune of $5,000,000 which one of the papers charges him with being possessed of, he has not now, nor did he ever have, belonging to him, separate from his wife, a single dollar's worth of property, and is today dependent upon his salary as a judge and the charity of his wife; and why these particular and atrocious charges at this particular time should be made with such boldness and audacity is a matter I hope you as grand jurors, whose duty it is, will look into, so that if you find them to be substantial, or even a suspicion that they are true, that you will give the judge a chance to resign. For infamy means one thing, and it ought to be ferreted out; and if a man or a newspaper editor will sit down deliberately and make a charge without any proof, let us see whether the rigor and terror of the law will not stop this thing in the future. For eleven years this judge has submitted to it without

new actions were commenced by them. In the first place, they sued the suers. Alleging the immense injury likely to result to the Erie Road from actions commenced, as they alleged, solely with a view of extorting money in settlement, Mr. Belmont was sued for a million of dollars in damages. Their second suit was against Messrs. Work, Schell, and others, concerned in the litigations of the previous spring, to recover the $429,250 then paid them, as was alleged, in a fraudulent settlement. These actions were, however, commonplace, and might have been brought by ordinary men. Messrs. Gould and Fisk were always displaying the invention of genius. The same day they carried their quarrels into the United States courts. The whole press, both of New York and of the country, disgusted with the parody of justice enacted in the State courts, had cried aloud to have the whole matter transferred to the United States tribunals, the decisions of

---

any notice, and now, having arrived at a period of life when his usefulness is impaired by such charges, he deems it his duty, and yours, gentlemen, to look into the matter whenever you have leisure, and say whether a combination of thieves, scoundrels, and rascals, who have infested Wall Street and Broad Street for years, and are now quarrelling among themselves, shall be permitted to turn around and endeavor to hide their own tracks by abuse and vilification of the judge."

It may be interesting to record how this fulmination affected the papers referred to. The Times the next morning commented on it as follows: "What we have said and done in the matter we have said and done deliberately; . . . . we believe we have said nothing that is not true, and nothing that cannot be proved to be true. At all events, we shall very willingly accept the responsibility of establishing its truth and of vindicating ourselves from the judge's imputations for having said it. A few days later it was reported that a true bill had been found against the Times, and that paper on the 26th congratulated the public on the fact. Finally, when Judge Barnard determined to drop the matter, the Times, in its issue of December 1, discoursed as follows on the subject: "We beg the judge to understand that we are quite ready to meet the issue that he tendered us, and to respond to such an indictment as he first urged the grand jury to find against us, or to a suit for damages, which would, perhaps, better suit the deplorable condition of pecuniary dependence to which he says he is reduced."

Nothing further came of the matter.

which might have some weight, and where, at least, no partisans upon the bench would shower each other with stays, injunctions, vacatings of orders, and other such pellets of the law. The Erie ring, as usual, took time by the forelock. While their slower antagonists were deliberating, they acted. On this Monday, the 23d, one Henry B. Whelpley, who had been a clerk of Gould's, and who claimed to be a stockholder in the Erie and a citizen of New Jersey, instituted a suit against the Erie Railway before Judge Blatchford, of the United States District Court. Alleging the doubts which hung over the validity of the recently issued stock, he petitioned that a receiver might be appointed, and the company directed to transfer into his hands enough property to secure from loss the plaintiff as well as all other holders of the new issues. The Erie counsel were on the ground, and, as soon as the petition was read, waived all further notice as to the matters contained in it; whereupon the court at once appointed Jay Gould receiver, and directed the Erie Company to place eight millions of dollars in his hands to protect the rights represented by the plaintiff. Of course the receiver was required to give bonds with sufficient sureties. Among the sureties was James Fisk, Jr. The brilliancy of this move was only surpassed by its success. It fell like a bombshell in the enemy's camp, and scattered dismay among those who still preserved a lingering faith in the virtue of law as administered by any known courts. The interference of the court was in this case asked for on the ground of fraud. If any fraud had been committed, the officers of the company alone could be the delinquents. To guard against the consequences of that fraud, a receivership was prayed for, and the court appointed as receiver the very officer in whom the alleged frauds, on which its action was based, must have originated. It is true, as was afterwards observed by Judge Nelson in setting it aside, that a *prima facie* case, for the appointment of a receiver "was supposed to have been made out," that no objection to the person suggested was made, and that the right was expressly reserved to other parties to come into court, with any allegations they saw fit against Receiver Gould. The collusion in the case was, nevertheless, so evident, the facts were so notorious and so apparent from the very papers before the court, and the character of Judge Blatchford is so far above suspicion, that it is hard to believe that this order was not procured from him by surprise, or through the agency of some counsel in whom he reposed a misplaced confidence. The Erie ring, at least, had no occasion to be dissatisfied with this day's proceedings.

The next day Judge Sutherland made short work of his brother Barnard's stay of proceedings in regard to the Davies receivership. He vacated it at once, and incontinently proceeded, wholly ignoring the action of Judge Blatchford on the day before, to settle the terms of the order, which, covering as it did the whole of the Erie property and franchise, excepting only the operating of the road, bade fair to lead to a conflict of jurisdiction between the State and Federal courts.

And now a new judicial combatant appears in the arena. It is difficult to say why Judge Barnard, at this time, disappears from the narrative. Perhaps the notorious judicial violence of the man, which must have made his eagerness as dangerous to the cause he espoused as the eagerness of a too swift witness, had alarmed the Erie counsel. Perhaps the fact that Judge Sutherland's term in chambers would expire in a few days had made them wish to intrust their cause to the magistrate who was to succeed him. At any rate, the new order staying proceedings under Judge Sutherland's order was obtained from Judge Cardozo,—it is said, somewhat before the terms of the receivership had been finally settled. The change spoke well for the discrimination of those who made it, for Judge Cardozo is a very different man from Judge Barnard. Courteous but inflexible, subtle, clear-headed, and unscrupulous, this magistrate conceals the iron hand beneath the silken glove. Equally versed in the laws of New York and in the mysteries of Tammany, he had earned his place by a partisan decision on the excise law, and was nominated for the bench by Mr. Fernando Wood, in a few remarks concluding as follows: "Judges were often called on to decide on political questions, and he was sorry to say the majority of them decided according to their political bias. It was therefore absolutely necessary to look to their candidate's political principles. He would nominate, as a fit man for the office of Judge of the Supreme Court, Albert Cardozo." Nominated as a partisan, a partisan Cardozo has always been, when the occasion demanded. Such was the new and far more formidable champion who now confronted Sutherland, in place of the vulgar Barnard. His first order in the matter—to show cause why the order of his brother judge should not be set aside—was not returnable until the 30th, and in the intervening five days many events were to happen.

Immediately after the settlement by Judge Sutherland of the order appointing Judge Davies receiver, that gentleman had proceeded to take possession of his trust. Upon arriving at the Erie building, he found it converted into a fortress, with a sentry patrolling behind the bolts and bars, to whom was confided the duty of scrutinizing all comers, and of admitting none but the faithful allies of the garrison. It so happened that Mr. Davies, himself unknown to the custodian, was accompanied by Mr. Eaton, the former attorney of the Erie corporation. This gentleman was recognized by the sentry, and forthwith the gates flew open for himself and his companion. In a few moments more the new receiver astonished Messrs. Gould and Fisk, and certain legal gentlemen with whom they happened to be in conference, by suddenly appearing in the midst of them. The apparition was not agreeable. Mr. Fisk, however, with a fair appearance of cordiality, welcomed the strangers, and shortly after left the room. Speedily returning, his manner underwent a change, and he requested the new-comers to go the way they came. As they did not comply at once, he opened the door, and directed their attention to some dozen men of forbidding aspect who stood outside, and who, he intimated, were prepared to eject them forcibly if they sought to prolong their unwelcome stay. As an indication of the lengths to which Mr. Fisk was prepared to go, this was sufficiently significant. The movement, however, was a little too rapid for his companions; the lawyers protested, Mr. Gould apologized, Mr. Fisk cooled down, and his familiars retired. The receiver then proceeded to give written notice of his appointment, and the fact that he had taken possession; disregarding, in so doing, an order of Judge Cardozo, staying proceedings under Judge Sutherland's order, which one of the opposing counsel drew from his pocket, but which Mr. Davies not inaptly characterized as a "very singular order," seeing that it was signed before the terms of the order it sought to affect were finally settled. At length, however, at the earnest request of some of the subordinate officials, and satisfied with the formal possession he had taken, the new receiver delayed further action until Friday. He little knew the resources of his opponents, if he vainly supposed that a formal possession signified anything. The succeeding Friday found the directors again fortified within, and himself a much enjoined wanderer without. The vigilant guards were now no longer to be beguiled. Within the building, constant discussions and consultations were taking place; without, relays of detectives incessantly watched the premises. No rumor was too wild for public credence. It was confidently stated that the directors were about to fly the State and the country,— that the treasury had already been conveyed to Canada. At last, late on Sunday night, Mr. Fisk with certain of his associates left the building, and made for the Jersey Ferry; but on the way he was stopped by a vigilant lawyer, and many papers were served upon him. His plans were then changed. He returned to the office of the company, and presently the detectives saw a carriage leave the Erie portals, and heard a loud voice order it to be driven to the Fifth Avenue Hotel. Instead of going there, however, it drove to the ferry, and presently an engine, with an empty directors' car attached, dashed out of the Erie station in Jersey City, and disappeared in the darkness. The detectives met and consulted; the carriage and the empty car were put together, and the inference, announced in every New York paper the succeeding day, was that Messrs. Fisk and Gould had absconded with millions of money to Canada.

That such a ridiculous story should have been published, much less believed, simply shows how utterly demoralized the public mind had become, and how prepared for any act of highhanded fraud or outrage. The libel did not long remain uncontradicted. The next day a card from Mr. Fisk was telegraphed to the newspapers, denying the calumny in indignant terms. The eternal steel rails were again made to do duty, and the midnight flitting became a harmless visit to Binghamton on business connected with a rolling-mill. Judge Balcom, however, of injunction memory in the earlier records of the Erie suits, resides at Binghamton, and a leading New York paper not inaptly made the timid inquiry of Mr. Fisk, "If he really thought that Judge Balcom was running a rolling-mill of the Erie Company, what did he think of Judge Barnard?" Mr. Fisk, however, as became him in his character of the Mæcenas of the bar, instituted suits claiming damages in fabulous sums, for defamation of character, against some half-dozen of the leading papers, and nothing further was heard of the matter, nor, indeed, of the suits either. Not so of the trip to Binghamton. On Tuesday, the 1st of December, while one set of lawyers were arguing an appeal in the Whelpley case before Judge Nelson in the Federal courts, and another set were procuring orders from Judge Cardozo staying proceedings authorized by Judge Sutherland, a third set were aiding Judge Balcom in certain new proceedings instituted in the name of the Attorney-General against the Erie Road. The result arrived at was, of course, that Judge Balcom declared his to be the only shop where a regular, reliable article in the way of law was retailed, and then proceeded forthwith to restrain and shut up the opposition establishments. The action was brought to terminate the existence of the defendant as a corporation, and, by way of preliminary, application was made for an injunction and the appointment of a receiver. His Honor held that, as only three receivers had as yet been appointed, he was certainly entitled to appoint another. It was perfectly clear to him that it was his duty to enjoin the defendant corporation from delivering the possession of its road, or of any of its assets, to either of the receivers already appointed; it was equally clear that the corporation would be obliged to deliver them to any receiver he might appoint. He was not prepared to name a receiver just then, however, though he intimated that he should not hesitate to do so if necessary. So he contented himself with the appointment of a referee to look into matters, and, generally, enjoined the directors from omitting to operate the road themselves, or from delivering the possession of it to "any person claiming to be a receiver."

This raiding upon the agricultural judges was not peculiar to the Erie party. On the contrary, in this proceeding it rather followed than set an example; for a day or two previous to Mr. Fisk's hurried journey, Judge Peckham of Albany had, upon papers identical with those in the Belmont suit, issued divers orders, similar to those of Judge Balcom, but on the other side, tying up the Erie directors in a most astonishing manner, and clearly hinting at the expediency of an additional receiver to be appointed at Albany. The amazing part of these Peckham and Balcom proceedings is, that they seem to have been initiated with perfect gravity, and neither to have been looked upon as jests, nor intended by their originators to bring the courts and the laws of New York into ridicule and contempt. Of course the several orders in these cases were of no more importance than so much waste paper, unless, indeed, some very cautious counsel may have considered an extra injunction or two very convenient things to have in his house; and yet, curiously enough, from a legal point of view, those in Judge Balcom's court seem to have been almost the only properly and regularly initiated proceedings in the whole case.

These little rural episodes in no way interfered with a renewal of vigorous hostilities in New York. While Judge Balcom was appointing his referee, Judge Cardozo granted an order for a reargument in the Belmont suit,—which brought up again the appointment of Judge Davies as receiver,—and assigned the hearing for the 6th of December. This step on his part bore a curious resemblance to certain of his performances in the notorious case of the Wood leases, and made the plan of operations perfectly clear. The period during which Judge Sutherland was to sit in chambers was to expire on the 4th of December, and Cardozo himself was to succeed him; he now, therefore, proposed to signalize his associate's departure from chambers by reviewing his orders. No sooner had he granted the motion, than the opposing counsel applied to Judge Sutherland, who forthwith issued an order to show cause why the reargument ordered by Judge Cardozo should not take place at once. Upon which the counsel of the Erie Road instantly ran over to Judge Cardozo, who vacated Judge Sutherland's order out of hand. The lawyers then left him and ran back to Judge Sutherland with a motion to vacate this last order. The contest was now becoming altogether too ludicrous. Somebody must yield, and when it was reduced to that, the honest Sutherland was pretty sure to give way to the subtle Cardozo. Accordingly the hearing on this last motion was postponed until the next morning, when Judge Sutherland made a not undignified statement as to his position, and closed by remitting the whole subject to the succeeding Monday, at which time Judge Cardozo was to succeed him in chambers. Cardozo, therefore, was now in undisputed possession of the field. In his closing explanation Judge Sutherland did not quote, as he might have done, the following excellent passage from the opinion of the court, of which both he and Cardozo were justices, delivered in the Schell case as recently as the last day of the previous June: "The idea that a cause, by such manœuvres as have been resorted to here, can be withdrawn from one judge of this court and taken possession of by another; that thus one judge of the same and no other powers can practically prevent his associate from exercising his judicial functions; that thus a case may be taken from judge to judge whenever one of the parties fears that an unfavorable decision is about to be rendered by the judge who, up to that time, had sat in the cause, and that thus a decision of a suit may be constantly indefinitely postponed at the will of one of the litigants, only deserves to be noticed as being a curiosity in legal tactics,—a remarkable exhibition of inventive genius and fertility of expedient to embarrass a suit which this extraordinarily conducted litigation has developed. . . . . Such a practice as that disclosed by this litigation, sanctioning the attempt to counteract the orders of each other in the progress of the suit, I confess is new and shocking to me, ... and I trust that we have seen the last in this high tribunal of such practices as this case has exhibited. No apprehension, real or fancied, that any judge is about, either wilfully or innocently, to do a wrong, can palliate, much less justify it." [18] Neither did Judge Sutherland state, as he might have stated, that this admirable expression of the sentiments of the full bench was written and delivered by Judge Albert Cardozo. Probably also Judge Cardozo and all his brother judges, rural and urban, as they used these bow-strings of the law, right and left,—as their reckless orders and injunctions struck deep into business circles far beyond the limits of their State,—as they degraded themselves in degrading their order, and made the ermine of supreme justice scarcely more imposing than the motley of the clown,— these magistrates may have thought that they had developed at least a novel, if not a respectable, mode of conducting litigation. They had not done even this. They had simply, so far as in them lay, turned back the wheels of progress and reduced the America of the nineteenth century to the level of the France of the sixteenth. "The advocates and judges of our times find bias enough in all causes to accommodate them to what they themselves think fit. . . . . What one court has determined one way another determines quite contrary, and itself contrary to that at another time; of which we see very frequent examples, owing to that practice admitted among us, and which is a marvellous blemish to the ceremonious authority and lustre of our justice, of not abiding

[18] *Schell* v. *Erie Railway Co.,* 51 Barbour's S. C. 373, 374.

by one sentence, but running from judge to judge, and court to court, to decide one and the same cause." [19]

It was now very clear that Receiver Davies might abandon all hope of operating the Erie Railway, and that Messrs. Gould and Fisk were borne upon the swelling tide of victory. The prosperous aspect of their affairs encouraged these last-named gentlemen to yet more vigorous offensive operations. The next attack was upon Vanderbilt in person. On Saturday, the 5th of December, only two days after Judge Sutherland and Receiver Davies were disposed of, the indefatigable Fisk waited on Commodore Vanderbilt, and, in the name of the Erie Company, tendered him fifty thousand shares of Erie common stock at 70.[20] As the stock was then selling in Wall Street at 40, the Commodore naturally declined to avail himself of this liberal offer. He even went further, and, disregarding his usual wise policy of silence, wrote to the New

[19] Montaigne's Works, Vol. II, p. 316.

[20] Throughout these proceedings glimpses are from time to time obtained of the more prominent characters in their undress, as it were, which have in them a good many elements both of nature and humor. The following description of the visit in which this tender was made was subsequently given by Fisk on the witness-stand: "I went to his (Vanderbilt's) house; it was a bad, stormy day, and I had the shares in a carpet-bag; I told the Commodore I had come to tender 50,000 shares of Erie and wanted back the money which we had paid for them and the bonds, and I made a separate demand for the $1,000,000 which had been paid to cover his losses; he said he had nothing to do with the Erie now, and must consult his counsel; . . . . Mr. Shearman was with me; the date I don't know; it was about eleven o'clock in the morning; don't know the day, don't know the month, don't know the year; I rode up with Shearman, holding the carpet-bag tight between my legs; I told him he was a small man and not much protection; this was dangerous property, you see, and might blow up; . . . . besides Mr. Shearman the driver went in with the witnesses, and besides the Commodore I spoke with the servant-girl; the Commodore was sitting on the bed with one shoe off and one shoe on; . . . . don't remember what more was said; I remember the Commodore put on his other shoe; I remember those shoes on account of the buckles; you see there were four buckles on that shoe, and I know it passed through my mind that if such men wore that kind of shoe I must get me a pair; this passed through my mind, but I did not speak of it to the Commodore; I was very civil to him."

York Times a short communication, in which he referred to the alleged terms of settlement of the previous July, so far as they concerned himself, and denied them in the following explicit language: "I have had no dealings with the Erie Railway Company, nor have I ever sold that company any stock or received from them any *bonus*. As to the suits instituted by Mr. Schell and others, I had nothing to do with them, nor was I in any way concerned in their settlement." This was certainly an announcement calculated to confuse the public; but the confusion became confounded, when, upon the 10th, Mr. Fisk followed him in a card in which he reiterated the alleged terms of settlement, and reproduced two checks of the Erie Company, of July 11, 1868, made payable to the treasurer and by him indorsed to C. Vanderbilt, upon whose order they had been paid. These two checks were for the sum of a million of dollars. He further said that the company had a paper in Mr. Vanderbilt's own handwriting, stating that he had placed fifty thousand shares of Erie stock in the hands of certain persons, to be delivered on payment of $3,500,000, which sum he declared had been paid. Undoubtedly these apparent discrepancies of statement admitted of an explanation; and some thin veil of equivocation, such as the transaction of the business through third parties, justified Vanderbilt's statements to his own conscience. Comment, however, is wholly superfluous, except to call attention to the amount of weight which is to be given to the statements and denials, apparently the most general and explicit, which from time to time were made by the parties to these proceedings. This short controversy merely added a little more discredit to what was already not deficient in that respect. On the 10th of December the Erie Company sued Commodore Vanderbilt for $3,500,000, specially alleging in their complaint the particulars of that settlement, all knowledge of or connection with which the defendant had so emphatically denied.

None of the multifarious suits which had been brought as yet were aimed at Mr. Drew. The quondam treasurer had apparently wholly disappeared from the scene on the 19th of November. Mr. Fisk took advantage, however, of a leisure day, to remedy this oversight, and a suit was commenced against Drew, on the ground of certain transactions between him, as treasurer, and the railway company, in relation to some steamboats concerned in the trade of Lake Erie. The usual allegations of fraud, breach of trust, and other trifling and, technically, not State prison offences, were made, and damages were set at a million of dollars.

Upon the 8th the argument in Belmont's case had been reopened before Judge Cardozo in New York, and upon the same day, in Oneida County, Judge Boardman, another justice of the Supreme Court, had proceeded to contribute his share to the existing complications. Counsel in behalf of Receiver Davies had appeared before him, and, upon their application, the Cardozo injunction, which restrained the receiver from taking possession of the Erie Railway, had been dissolved. Why this application was made, or why it was granted, surpasses comprehension. However, the next day, Judge Boardman's order having been read in court before Judge Cardozo, that magistrate suddenly revived to a full appreciation of the views expressed by him in June in regard to judicial interference with judicial action, and at once stigmatized Judge Boardman's action as "extremely indecorous." Neglecting, however, the happy opportunity to express an opinion as to his own conduct during the previous week, he simply stayed all proceedings under this new order, and applied himself to the task of hearing the case before him reargued.

This hearing lasted many days, was insufferably long and inexpressibly dull. While it was going on, upon the 15th, Judge Nelson, in the United States Court, delivered his opinion in the Whelpley suit, reversing, on certain technical grounds, the action of Judge Blatchford, and declaring that no case for the appointment of a receiver had been made out; accordingly he set aside that of Gould, and, in conclusion, sent the matter back to the State court, or, in other words, to Judge Cardozo, for decision. Thus the gentlemen of the ring, having been most fortunate in getting their case into the Federal court before Judge Blatchford, were now even more fortunate in getting it out of that court when it had come before Judge Nelson. After this, room for doubt no longer existed. Brilliant success at every point had crowned the strategy of the Erie directors. For once Vanderbilt was effectually routed and driven from the field. That he shrunk from continuing the contest against such opponents is much to his credit. It showed that he, at least, was not prepared to see how near he could come to the doors of a State prison and yet not enter them; that he did not care to take in advance the opinion of leading counsel as to whether what he meant to do might place him in the felons' dock. Thus Erie was wholly given over to the control of the ring. No one seemed any longer to dispute their right and power to issue as much new stock as might seem to them expedient. Injunctions had failed to check them; receivers had no terrors for them. Secure in their power, they now extended their operations over sea and land, leasing railroads, buying steamboats, ferries, theatres, and rolling-mills, building connecting links of road, laying down additional rails, and, generally, proving themselves a power wherever corporations were to be influenced or legislatures were to be bought.

Christmas, the period of peace and good-will, was now approaching. The dreary arguments before Judge Cardozo had terminated on December 18, long after the press and the public had ceased to pay any attention to them, and already rumors of a settlement were rife. Yet it was not meet that the settlement should be effected without some final striking catastrophe, some characteristic concluding tableau. Among the many actions which had incidentally sprung from these proceedings was one against Mr. Samuel Bowles, the editor of the Springfield Republican, brought by Mr. Fisk in consequence of an article which had appeared in that paper, reflecting most severely on Fisk's proceedings and private character,—his past, his present, and his probable future. On the 22d of December, Mr. Bowles happened to be in New York, and, as he was standing in the office of his hotel, talking with a friend, was suddenly arrested on the warrant of Judge McCunn, hurried into a carriage, and driven to Ludlow Street Jail, where he was locked up for the night. This excellent jest afforded intense amusement, and was the cause of much wit that evening at an entertainment given by the Tammany ring to the newly elected mayor of New York, at which entertainment Mr. James Fisk, Jr., was an honored guest. The next morning the whole press was in a state of high indignation, and Mr. Bowles had suddenly become the best-advertised editor in the country. At an early hour he was, of course, released on bail, and with this outrage the second Erie contest was brought to a close. It seemed right and proper that proceedings which, throughout, had set public opinion at defiance, and in which the Stock Exchange, the courts, and the legislature had come in for equal measures of opprobrium for their disregard of private rights, should be terminated by an exhibition of petty spite, in which bench and bar, judge, sheriff, and jailer, lent themselves with base subserviency to a violation of the liberty of the citizen.

It was not until the 10th of February that Judge Cardozo published his decision setting aside the Sutherland receivership, and establishing on a basis of authority the right to over-issue stock at pleasure. The subject was then as obsolete and forgotten as though it had never absorbed the public attention. And another "settlement" had already been effected. The details of this arrangement have not been dragged to light through the exposures of subsequent litigation. But it is not difficult to see where and how a combination of overpowering influence may have been effected, and a guess might even be hazarded as to its objects and its victims. The fact that a settlement had been arrived at was intimated in the papers of the 26th of December. On the 19th of the same month a stock dividend of eighty per cent in the New York Central had been suddenly declared by Vanderbilt. Presently the legislature met. While the Erie ring seemed to have good reasons for apprehending hostile legislation, Vanderbilt, on his part, might have feared for the success of a bill which was to legalize his new stock. But hardly a voice was raised against the Erie men, and the bill of the Central was safely carried through. This curious absence of opposition did not stop here, and soon the two parties were seen united in an active alliance. Vanderbilt wanted to consolidate his roads; the Erie directors wanted to avoid the formality of annual elections. Thereupon two other bills went hastily through this honest and patriotic legislature, the one authorizing the Erie Board, which had been elected for one year, to classify itself so that one fifth only of its members should vacate office during each succeeding year, the other consolidating the Vanderbilt roads into one colossal monopoly. Public interests and private rights seem equally to have been the victims. It is impossible to say that the beautiful unity of interests which led to such results was the fulfilment of the December settlement; but it is a curious fact that the same paper which announced in one column that Vanderbilt's two measures, known as the consolidation and Central scrip bills had gone to the Governor for signature, should, in another, have reported the discontinuance of the Belmont and Whelpley suits by the consent of all interested.[21] It may be that public and private interests were not thus balanced and traded away in a servile legislature, but the strong probabilities are that the settlement of December made white even that of July. Meanwhile the conquerors—the men whose names had been made notorious through the whole land in all these infamous proceedings—were at last undisputed masters of the situation, and no man questioned the firmness of their grasp on the Erie Railway. They walked erect and proud of their infamy through the streets of our great cities; they voluntarily subjected themselves to that to which other depredators are compelled to submit, and, by exposing their portraits in public conveyances, converted noble steamers into branch galleries of a police-office; nay, more, they bedizened their persons with gold lace, and assumed honored titles, until those who witnessed in silent contempt their strange antics were disposed to exclaim

21 See the New York Tribune of May 10, 1869.

94

in the language of poor Doll Tearsheet: "An Admiral! God's light, these villains will make the word as odious as the word 'occupy,' which was an excellent good word before it was ill sorted; therefore, Admirals had need look to 't."

The subsequent history of the Erie Railway, under the management of the men who had thus succeeded in gaining absolute control over it, forms no part of this narrative. The attempt has been made simply to trace the course of events which resulted in placing a national thoroughfare in the hands of unscrupulous gamblers, and to describe the complications which marked their progress to power. The end was finally attained, when, after every opponent had, by fair means or by foul, been driven from the conflict, that strange law was enacted which assured these men, elected for one year, a five years' term of power, beyond the control of their stockholders. From that moment all the great resources of the Erie Railway became mere engines with which to work their lawless will.

Comment would only weaken the force of this narrative. It sufficiently suggests its own moral. The facts which have been set forth cannot but have revealed to every observant eye the deep decay which has eaten into our social edifice. No portion of our system was left untested, and no portion showed itself to be sound. The stock exchange revealed itself as a haunt of gamblers and a den of thieves; the offices of our great corporations appeared as the secret chambers in which trustees plotted the spoliation of their wards; the law became a ready engine for the furtherance of wrong, and the ermine of the judge did not conceal the eagerness of the partisan; the halls of legislation were transformed into a mart in which the price of votes was higgled over, and laws, made to order, were bought and sold; while under all, and through all, the voice of public opinion was silent or was disregarded.

It is not, however, in connection with the present that all this has its chief significance. It speaks ominously for the future. It may be that our society is only passing through a period of ugly transition, but the present evil has its root deep down in the social organization, and springs from a diseased public opinion. Failure seems to be regarded as the one unpardonable crime, success as the all-redeeming virtue, the acquisition of wealth as the single worthy aim of life. Ten years ago such revelations as these of the Erie Railway would have sent a shudder through the community, and would have placed a stigma on every man who had had to do with them. Now they merely incite others to surpass them by yet bolder outrages and more corrupt combinations. Were this not so, these things would be as impossible among us now as they are elsewhere, or as they were here not many years ago. While this continues it is mere weakness to attribute the consequences of a lax morality to a defective currency, or seek to prevent its outward indications by statute remedies. The root of the disease is deep; external applications will only hide its dangerous symptoms. It is well to reform the currency, it is well to enact laws against malefactors; but neither the one nor the other will restore health to a business community which tolerates successful fraud, or which honors wealth more than honesty.

One leading feature of these developments, however, is, from its political aspect, especially worthy of the attention of the American people. Modern society has created a class of artificial beings who bid fair soon to be the masters of their creator. It is but a very few years since the existence of a corporation controlling a few millions of dollars was regarded as a subject of grave apprehension, and now this country already contains single organizations which wield a power represented by hundreds of millions. These bodies are the creatures of single States; but in New York, in Pennsylvania, in Maryland, in New Jersey, and not in those States alone, they are already establishing despotisms which no spasmodic popular effort will be able to shake off. Everywhere, and at all times, however, they illustrate the truth of the old maxim of the common law, that corporations have no souls. Only in New York has any intimation yet been given of what the future may have in store for us should these great powers become mere tools in the hands of ambitious, reckless men. The system of corporate life and corporate power, as applied to industrial development, is yet in its infancy. It tends always to development,—always to consolidation,—it is ever grasping new powers, or insidiously exercising covert influence. Even now the system threatens the central government. The Erie Railway represents a weak combination compared to those which day by day are consolidating under the unsuspecting eyes of the community. A very few years more, and we shall see corporations as much exceeding the Erie and the New York Central in both ability and will for corruption as they will exceed those roads in wealth and in length of iron track. We shall see these great corporations spanning the continent from ocean to ocean,—single, consolidated lines, not connecting Albany with Buffalo, or Lake Erie with the Hudson, but uniting the Atlantic and the Pacific, and bringing New York nearer to San Francisco than Albany once was to Buffalo. Already the disconnected members of these future leviathans have built up States in the wilderness, and chosen their attorneys senators of the United States. Now their power is in its infancy; in a very few years they will re-enact, on a larger theatre and on a grander scale, with every feature magnified, the scenes which were lately witnessed on the narrow stage of a single State. The public corruption is the foundation on which corporations always depend for their political power. There is a natural tendency to coalition between them and the lowest strata of political intelligence and morality; for their agents must obey, not question. They exact success, and do not cultivate political morality. The lobby is their home, and the lobby thrives as political virtue decays. The ring is their symbol of power, and the ring is the natural enemy of political purity and independence. All this was abundantly illustrated in the events which have just been narrated. The existing coalition between the Erie Railway and the Tammany ring is a natural one, for the former needs votes, the latter money. This combination now controls the legislature and courts of New York; that it controls also the Executive of the

State, as well as that of the city, was proved when Governor Hoffman recorded his reasons for signing the infamous Erie Directors' Bill. It is a new power, for which our language contains no name. We know what aristocracy, autocracy, democracy are; but we have no word to express government by moneyed corporations. Yet the people already instinctively seek protection against it, and look for such protection, significantly enough, not to their own legislatures, but to the single autocratic feature retained in our system of government, —the veto by the Executive. In this there is something more imperial than republican. The people have lost faith in themselves when they cease to have any faith in those whom they uniformly elect to represent them. The change that has taken place in this respect of late years in America has been startling in its rapidity. Legislation is more and more falling into contempt, and this not so much on account of the extreme ignorance manifested in it as because of the corrupt motives which are believed habitually to actuate it. Thus the influence of corporations and of class interests is steadily destroying that belief in singleness of purpose which alone enables a representative government to exist, and the community is slowly accustoming itself to look for protection, not to public opinion, but to some man in high place and armed with great executive powers. Him they now think they can hold to some accountability. It remains to be seen what the next phase in this process of gradual development will be. History never quite repeats itself, and, as was suggested in the first pages of this narrative, the old familiar enemies may even now confront us, though arrayed in such a modern garb that no suspicion is excited. Americans are apt pupils, and among them there are probably some who have not observed Fisk and Vanderbilt and Hoffman without a thought of bettering their instructions. No successful military leader will repeat in America the threadbare experiences of Europe;—the executive power is not likely to be seized while the legislative is suppressed. The indications would now seem rather to point towards the corruption of the legislative and a quiet assumption of the executive through some combination in one vigorous hand of those influences which throughout this narrative have been seen only in conflict. As the Erie ring represents the combination of the corporation and the hired proletariat of a great city; as Vanderbilt embodies the autocratic power of Cæsarism introduced into corporate life, and as neither alone can obtain complete control of the government of the State, it, perhaps, only remains for the coming man to carry the combination of elements one step in advance, and put Cæsarism at once in control of the corporation and of the proletariat, to bring our vaunted institutions within the rule of all historic precedent.

It is not pleasant to take such views of the future; yet they are irresistibly suggested by the events which have been narrated. They seem to be in the nature of direct inferences. The only remedy lies in a renovated public opinion; but no indication of this has as yet been elicited. People did indeed, at one time, watch these Erie developments with interest, but the feeling excited was rather one of amazement than of indignation. Even where a real indignation was excited, it led to no sign of any persistent effort at reform; it betrayed itself only in aimless denunciation or in sad forebodings. The danger, however, is day by day increasing, and the period during which the work of regeneration should begin grows always shorter. It is true that evils ever work their own cure, but the cure for the evils of Roman civilization was worked out through ten centuries of barbarism. It remains to be seen whether this people retains that moral vigor which can alone awaken a sleeping public opinion to healthy and persistent activity, or whether to us also will apply these words of the latest and best historian of the Roman republic: "What Demosthenes said of his Athenians was justly applied to the Romans of this period; that people were very zealous for action so long as they stood round the platform and listened to proposals of reform; but, when they went home, no one thought further of what he had heard in the market-place. However those reformers might stir the fire, it was to no purpose, for the inflammable material was wanting." [22]

[22] Mommsen, Vol. IV, p. 91, referring to the early Ciceronian period, B.C. 75.

The New York Gold Conspiracy

House of Representatives. Report, No. 31. Forty-first Congress, Second Session. Report of the Committee on Banking and Currency, in response to a Resolution of the House of Representatives, passed December 13, 1869, directing the Committee "to investigate the causes that led to the unusual and extraordinary fluctuations of Gold in the City of New York, from the 21st to the 27th of September, 1869"; accompanied by the Testimony collected by the Committee.

THE civil war in America, with its enormous issues of depreciating currency, and its reckless waste of money and credit by the government, created a speculative mania such as the United States, with all its experience in this respect, had never before known. Not only in Broad Street, the centre of New York speculation, but far and wide throughout the Northern States, almost every man who had money at all employed a part of his capital in the purchase of stocks or of gold, of copper, of petroleum, or of domestic produce, in the hope of a rise in prices, or staked money on the expectation of a fall. To use the jargon of the street, every farmer and every shopkeeper in the country seemed to be engaged in "carrying" some favorite security "on a margin." Whoever could obtain five pounds sent it to a broker with orders to buy fifty pounds' worth of stocks, or whatever amount the broker would consent to purchase. If the stock rose, the speculator prospered; if it fell until the five pounds of deposit or margin were lost, the broker demanded a new deposit, or sold the stock to protect himself. By means of this simple and smooth machinery, which differs in no essential respect from the processes of *roulette* or *rouge-et-noir,* the whole nation flung itself into the Stock Exchange, until the "outsiders," as they were called, in opposition to the regular brokers of Broad Street, represented nothing less than the entire population of the American Republic. Every one speculated, and for a time every one speculated successfully.

The inevitable reaction began when the government, about a year after the close of the war, stopped its issues and ceased borrowing. The greenback currency had for a moment sunk to a value of only 37 cents to the dollar. It is even asserted that on the worst day of all, the 11th of July, 1864, one sale of £20,000 in gold was actually made at 310, which is equivalent to about 33 cents in the dollar.[1] At this point, however, the depreciation stopped; and the paper which had come so near falling into entire discredit steadily rose in value, first to 50 cents, then to 60, to 70, and within the present year to more than 90 cents. So soon as the industrious part of the public felt the touch of this return to solid values, the whole fabric of fictitious wealth began to melt away under their eyes.

Thus it was not long before the so-called "outsiders," the men who speculated on their own account, and could not act in agreement or combination, began to suffer. One by one, or in great masses, they were made the prey of the larger operators; their last margins were consumed, and they dropped down to the solid level of slow, productive industry. Some lost everything; many lost still more than they had, and there are few families of ordinary connection and standing in the United States which cannot tell, if they choose, some dark

[1] See Men and Mysteries of Wall Street, by James K. Medbery, pp. 250, 251.

story of embezzlement, or breach of trust, committed in these days. Some men, who had courage and a sense of honor, found life too heavy for them; others went mad. But the greater part turned in silence to their regular pursuits, and accepted their losses as they could. Almost every rich American could produce from some pigeon-hole a bundle of worthless securities, and could show check-books representing the only remaining trace of margin after margin consumed in vain attempts to satisfy the insatiable broker. A year or two of incessant losses swept the weaker gamblers from the street.

But even those who continued to speculate found it necessary to change their mode of operations. Chance no longer ruled over the Stock Exchange and the gold market. The fate of a battle, the capture of a city, or the murder of a President, had hitherto been the influences which broke through the plans of the strongest combinations, and put all speculators, whether great or small, on fairly even ground; but as the period of sudden and uncontrollable disturbing elements passed away, the market fell more and more completely into the hands of cliques which found a point of adhesion in some great mass of incorporated capital. Three distinct railways, with all their enormous resources, became the property of Cornelius Vanderbilt, who, by means of their credit and capital, again and again swept millions of dollars into his pocket by a process curiously similar to gambling with loaded dice. But Vanderbilt was one of the most respectable of these great operators. The Erie Railway was controlled by Daniel Drew, and while Vanderbilt at least acted in the interests of his corporations, Drew cheated equally his corporation and the public. Between these two men and the immense incorporated power they swayed, smaller operators, one after another, were crushed to pieces, until the survivors learned to seek shelter within some clique sufficiently strong to afford protection. Speculation in this manner began to consume itself, and the largest combination of capital was destined to swallow every weaker combination which ventured to show it itself in the market.

Thus, between the inevitable effect of a currency which steadily shrank the apparent wealth of the country, and the omnipotence of capital in the stock market, a sounder and healthier state of society began to make itself felt. Nor could the unfortunate public, which had been robbed with such cynical indifference by Drew and Vanderbilt, feel any sincere regret when they saw these two cormorants reduced to tearing each other. In the year 1867 Mr. Vanderbilt undertook to gain possession of the Erie Road, as he had already obtained possession of the New York Central, the second trunk line between New York and the West. Mr. Vanderbilt was supposed to own property to the value of some £10,000,000, all of which might be made directly available for stock operations. He bought the greater part of the Erie stock; Drew sold him all he could take, and then issued as much more as was required in order to defeat Vanderbilt's purpose. After a violent struggle, which overthrew all the guaranties of social order, Drew triumphed, and Mr. Vanderbilt abandoned the contest. The Erie corporation paid him a large sum to reimburse his alleged losses. At the same time it was agreed that Mr. Drew's accounts should be passed, and he obtained a release in full, and retired from the direction. And the Erie Road, almost exhausted by such systematic plundering, was left in the undisturbed, if not peaceful, control of Mr. Jay Gould and Mr. James Fisk, Jr., whose reign began in the month of July, 1868.

Mr. Jay Gould was a partner in the firm of Smith, Gould, & Martin, brokers, in Wall Street. He had been engaged before now in railway enterprises, and his operations had not been of a nature likely to encourage public confidence in his ideas of fiduciary relations. He was a broker, and a broker is almost by nature a gambler, perhaps the very last profession suitable for a railway manager. In character he was strongly marked by his disposition for silent intrigue. He preferred as a rule to operate on his own account, without admitting other persons into his confidence, and he seemed never to be satisfied except when deceiving every one as to his intentions. There was a reminiscence of the spider in his nature. He spun huge webs, in corners and in the dark, which were seldom strong enough to resist a serious strain at the critical moment. His disposition to this subtlety and elaboration of intrigue was irresistible. It is scarcely necessary to say that he had not a conception of a moral principle. In speaking of this class of men it must be fairly assumed at the outset that they do not and cannot understand how there can be a distinction between right and wrong in matters of speculation, so long as the daily settlements are punctually effected. In this respect Mr. Gould was probably as honest as the mass of his fellows, according to the moral standard of the street; but without entering upon technical questions of roguery, it is enough to say that he was an uncommonly fine and unscrupulous intriguer, skilled in all the processes of stock-gambling, and passably indifferent to the praise or censure of society.

James Fisk, Jr., was still more original in character. He was not yet forty years of age, and had the instincts of fourteen. He came originally from Vermont, probably the most respectable and correct State in the Union, and his father had been a pedler who sold goods from town to town in his native valley of the Connecticut. The son followed his father's calling with boldness and success. He drove his huge wagon, made resplendent with paint and varnish, with four or six horses, through the towns of Vermont and Western Massachusetts; and when his father remonstrated in alarm at his reckless management, the young man, with his usual bravado, took his father into his service at a fixed salary, with the warning that he was not to put on airs on the strength of his new dignity. A large Boston firm which had supplied his goods on credit, attracted by his energy, took him into the house; the war broke out; his influence drew the firm into some bold speculations which were successful; in a few years he retired with some £20,000, which he subsequently lost. He formed a connection with Daniel Drew in New York, and a new sign, ominous of future trouble, was raised in Wall Street, bearing the names of Fisk & Belden, brokers.

Personally Mr. Fisk was coarse, noisy, boastful, ignorant; the type of a young butcher in appearance and mind. Nothing could be more striking than the contrast between him and his future associate Gould. One was small and slight in person, dark, sallow, reticent, and stealthy, with a trace of Jewish origin. The other was large, florid, gross, talkative, and obstreperous. Mr. Fisk's redeeming point was his humor, which had a strong flavor of American nationality. His mind was extraordinarily fertile in ideas and expedients, while his conversation was filled with unusual images and strange forms of speech, which were caught up and made popular by the New York press. In respect to honesty as between Gould and Fisk, the latter was, perhaps, if possible, less deserving of trust than the former. A story not without a keen stroke of satirical wit is told by him, which illustrates his estimate of abstract truth. An old woman who had bought of the elder Fisk a handkerchief which cost ninepence in the New England currency, where six shillings are reckoned to the dollar, complained to Mr. Fisk, Jr., that his father had cheated her. Mr. Fisk considered the case maturely, and gave a decision based on *a priori* principles. "No!" said he, "the old man wouldn't have told a lie for ninepence"; and then, as if this assertion needed some reasonable qualification, he added, "though he would have told eight of them for a dollar!" The distinction as regards the father may have been just, since the father seems to have held old-fashioned ideas as to wholesale and retail trade; but in regard to the son even this relative degree of truth cannot be predicated with any confidence, since, if the Investigating Committee of Congress and its evidence are to be believed, Mr. Fisk seldom or never speaks truth at all.

An intrigue equally successful and disreputable brought these two men into the Erie Board of Directors, whence they speedily drove their more timid predecessor Drew. In July, 1868, Gould made himself President and Treasurer of the corporation. Fisk became Comptroller. A young lawyer, named Lane, became counsel. These three directors made a majority of the Executive Committee, and were masters of Erie. The

Board of Directors held no meetings. The Executive Committee was never called together, and the three men—Fisk, Gould, and Lane—became from this time the absolute, irresponsible owners of the Erie Railway, not less than if it had been their personal property and plaything.

This property was in effect, like all the great railway corporations, an empire within a republic. It consisted of a trunk line of road 459 miles in length, with branches 314 miles in extent, or 773 miles of road in all. Its capital stock amounted to about £7,000,000. Its gross receipts exceeded £3,000,000 per annum. It employed not less than 15,000 men, and supported their families. Over all this wealth and influence, greater than that directly swayed by any private citizen, greater than is absolutely and personally controlled by most kings, and far too great for the public safety either in a democracy or in any other form of society, the vicissitudes of a troubled time placed two men in irresponsible authority; and both these men belonged to a low and degraded moral and social type. Such an elevation has been rarely seen in modern history. Even the most dramatic of modern authors, even Balzac himself, who so loved to deal with similar violent alternations of fortune, or Alexandre Dumas, with all his extravagance of imagination, never have reached a conception bolder or more melodramatic than this, nor have they ever ventured to conceive a plot so enormous, or a catastrophe so original, as was now to be developed.

One of the earliest acts of the new rulers was precisely such as Balzac or Dumas might have predicted and delighted in. They established themselves in a palace. The old offices of the Erie Railway were in the lower part of the city, among the wharves and warehouses; a situation, no doubt, convenient for business, but by no means agreeable as a residence; and the new proprietors naturally wished to reside on their property. Mr. Fisk and Mr. Gould accordingly bought a huge building of white marble, not unlike a European palace, situated about two miles from the business quarter, and containing a large theatre or opera-house. They also purchased several smaller houses adjoining it. The opera-house cost about £140,000, and a large part of the building was at once leased, by the two purchasers, to themselves as the Erie corporation, to serve as offices. This suite of apartments was then furnished by themselves, as representing the corporation, at an expense of some £60,000, and in a style which, though called vulgar, is certainly not more vulgar than that of the President's official residence, and which would be magnificent in almost any palace in Europe. The adjoining houses were connected with the main building; and in one of these Mr. Fisk had his private apartments, with a private passage to his opera-box. He also assumed direction of the theatre, of which he became manager-in-chief. To these royal arrangements he brought tastes which have been commonly charged as the worst results of royal license. The atmosphere of the Erie offices was not supposed to be disturbed with moral prejudices; and as the opera itself supplied Mr. Fisk's mind with amusement, so the opera *troupe* supplied him with a permanent harem. Whatever Mr. Fisk did was done on an extraordinary scale.

These arrangements, however, regarded only the pleasures of the American Aladdin. In the conduct of their interests the new directors showed a capacity for large conceptions, and a vigor in the execution of their schemes, such as alarmed the entire community. At the annual election in 1868, when Gould, Fisk, and Lane, having borrowed or bought proxies for the greater part of the stock, caused themselves to be elected for the ensuing year, the respectable portion of the public throughout the country was astonished and shocked to learn that the new Board of Directors contained two names peculiarly notorious and obnoxious to honest men,—the names of William M. Tweed and Peter B. Sweeney. To English ears these commonplace, not to say vulgar, titles do not seem singularly alarming; but to every honest American they conveyed a peculiar sense of terror and disgust. The State of New York in its politics is much influenced, if not controlled, by the city of New York. The city politics are so entirely in the hands of the Democratic party as to preclude even the existence of a strong minority. The party organization centres in a political club, held together by its patronage and the money it controls through a system of jobbery unequalled elsewhere in the world. And the Tammany Club, thus swaying the power of a small nation of several million souls, is itself ruled by William M. Tweed and Peter B. Sweeney, absolute masters of this terrible system of theft and fraud, and to American eyes the incarnation of political immorality.

The effect of this alliance was felt in the ensuing winter in the passage of a bill through the State legislature, and its signature by the Governor, abolishing the former system of annual elections of the entire board of Erie directors, and authorizing the board to classify itself in such a manner that only a portion should be changed each year. The principle of the bill was correct. Its practical effect, however, was to enable Gould and Fisk to make themselves directors for five years, in spite of any attempt on the part of the stockholders to remove them. The formality of annual re-election was spared them; and so far as the stockholders were concerned, there was no great injustice in the act. The Erie Road was in the peculiar position of being without an owner. There was no *cestui que trust,* unless the English stockholders could be called such. In America the stock was almost exclusively held for speculation, not for investment; and in the morals of Wall Street speculation means, or had almost come to mean, disregard of intrinsic value. In this case society at large was the injured party, and society knew its risk.

This step, however, was only a beginning. The Tammany ring, as it is called, exercised a power far beyond politics. Under the existing constitution of the State, the judges of the State courts are elected by the people. There are thirty-three such judges in New York, and each of the thirty-three is clothed with equity powers running through the whole State. Of these judges Tammany Hall elected several, and the Erie Railway controlled others in country districts. Each of these judges might forbid proceedings before any and all the other judges, or stay proceedings in suits already commenced. Thus the lives and the property of the public were in the power of the new combination; and two of the city judges, Barnard and Cardozo, had already acquired a peculiarly infamous reputation as so-called "slaves to the ring," which left no question as to the depths to which their prostitution of justice would descend.

The alliance between Tammany and Erie was thus equivalent to investing Mr. Gould and Mr. Fisk with the highest attributes of sovereignty; but in order to avail themselves to the utmost of their judicial powers, they also required the ablest legal assistance. The degradation of the bench had been rapidly followed by the degradation of the bar. Prominent and learned lawyers were already accustomed to avail themselves of social or business relations with judges to forward private purposes. One whose partner might be elevated to the bench was certain to be generally retained in cases brought before this special judge; and litigants were taught by experience that a retainer in such cases was profitably bestowed. Others found a similar advantage resulting from known social relations with the court. The debasement of tone was not confined to the lower ranks of advocates; and it was probably this steady demoralization of the bar which made it possible for the Erie ring to obtain the services of Mr. David Dudley Field as its legal adviser. Mr. Field, a gentleman of European reputation, in regard to which he is understood to be peculiarly solicitous, was an eminent law reformer, author of the New York Code, delegate of the American Social Science Association to the European International Congress, and asserted by his partner, Mr. Shearman, in evidence before a committee of the New York legislature, to be a man of quixotic sense of honor. Mr. Shearman himself, a gentleman of English parentage, had earned public gratitude by arraigning and deploring, with unsurpassed courage and point, the condition of the New York judiciary, in an admirable essay which will be found in the North American Review for July, 1867. The value of Mr. Field's services to

Messrs. Fisk and Gould was not to be measured even by the enormous fees their generosity paid him. His power over certain judges became so absolute as to impress the popular imagination; and the gossip of Wall Street insists that he has a silken halter round the neck of Judge Barnard, and a hempen one round that of Cardozo. It is certain that he who had a year before threatened Barnard on his own bench with impeachment now appeared in the character of Barnard's master, and issued as a matter of course the edicts of his court.

One other combination was made by the Erie managers to extend their power, and this time it was credit that was threatened. They bought a joint-stock bank in New York City, with a capital of £200,000. The assistance thus gained was purchased at a very moderate price, since it was by no means represented by the capital. The great cliques and so-called "operators" of Wall Street and Broad Street carry on their transactions by a system of credits and clearing-houses with a very limited use of money. The banks certify their checks, and the certified checks settle all balances. Nominally and by law the banks only certify to the extent of *bona fide* deposits, but in reality the custom of disregarding the strict letter of the law is not unknown, and in regard to the bank in question, the Comptroller of the Currency, an officer of the National Treasury, testifies that on an examination of its affairs in April, 1869, out of fifteen checks deposited in its hands as security for certifications made by it, selected at hazard for inquiry, and representing a nominal value of £300,000, three only were good. The rest represented accommodation extended to brokers and speculators without security. As an actual fact it is in evidence that this same bank on Thursday, September 24, 1869, certified checks to the amount of nearly £1,500,000 for Mr. Gould alone. What sound security Mr. Gould deposited against this mass of credit may be left to the imagination. His operations, however, were not confined to this bank alone, although this was the only one owned by the ring.

Thus Mr. Gould and Mr. Fisk created a combination more powerful than any that has been controlled by mere private citizens in America or in Europe since society for self-protection established the supreme authority of the judicial name. They exercised the legislative and the judicial powers of the State; they possessed almost unlimited credit, and society was at their mercy. One authority alone stood above them, beyond their control; and this was the distant but threatening figure of the National Government.

Nevertheless, powerful as they were, the Erie managers were seldom in funds. The huge marble palace in which they lived, the theatre which they supported, the reckless bribery and profusion of management by which they could alone maintain their defiance of public opinion, the enormous schemes for extending their operations into which they rushed with utter recklessness, all required greater resources than could be furnished even by the wholesale plunder of the Erie Road. They were obliged from time to time to issue from their castle and harry the industrious public or their brother freebooters. The process was different from that known to the dark ages, but the objects and the results were equally robbery. At one time Mr. Fisk is said to have ordered heavy speculative sales of stock in an express company which held a contract with the Erie Railway. The sales being effected, the contract was declared annulled. The stock naturally fell, and Mr. Fisk realized the difference. He then ordered heavy purchases, and having renewed the contract the stock rose again, and Mr. Fisk a second time swept the street.[2] In the summer and autumn of 1869 the two managers issued and sold 235,000 new shares of Erie stock, or nearly as much as its entire capital when they assumed power in July, 1868. With the aid of the money thus obtained, they succeeded in withdrawing about £2,500,000 in currency from circulation at the very moment of the year when currency was most in demand in order to harvest the crops. For weeks the whole nation writhed and quivered under the torture of this modern rack, until the

[2] Men and Mysteries of Wall Street, p. 168.

national government itself was obliged to interfere and threaten a sudden opening of the treasury. But whether the Erie speculators operated for a rise or operated for a fall, whether they bought or sold, and whether they were engaged in manipulating stocks, or locking up currency, or cornering gold, they were always a public nuisance and scandal.

In order to explain the operation of a so-called corner in gold to ordinary readers with the least possible use of slang or technical phrases, two preliminary statements are necessary. In the first place it must be understood that the supply of gold immediately available for transfers is limited within distinct bounds in America. New York and the country behind it contain an amount usually estimated at about £4,000,000. The national government commonly holds from £15,000,000 to £20,000,000, which may be thrown bodily on the market if the President orders it. To obtain gold from Europe or other sources requires time.

In the second place, gold in America is a commodity bought and sold like stocks in a special market or gold-room which is situated next the Stock Exchange in Broad Street and is practically a part of it. In gold as in stocks, the transactions are both real and speculative. The real transactions are mostly purchases or loans made by importers who require coin to pay customs on their imports. This legitimate business is supposed to require from £1,000,000 to £1,500,000 per day. The speculative transactions are mere wagers on the rise or fall of price, and neither require any actual transfer of gold, nor even imply its existence, although in times of excitement hundreds of millions nominally are bought, sold, and loaned.

Under the late administration Mr. McCulloch, the Secretary of the Treasury, had thought it his duty at least to guarantee a stable currency, although Congress forbade him to restore the gold standard. During four years gold had fluctuated little, and principally from natural causes, and the danger of attempting to create an artificial scarcity in it had prevented the operators from trying an experiment which would have been sure to irritate the government. The financial policy of the new administration was not so definitely fixed, and the success of a speculation would depend on the action of Mr. Boutwell, the new secretary, whose direction was understood to have begun by a marked censure on the course pursued by his predecessor.

Of all financial operations, cornering gold is the most brilliant and the most dangerous, and possibly the very hazard and splendor of the attempt were the reasons of its fascination to Mr. Jay Gould's fancy. He dwelt upon it for months, and played with it like a pet toy. His fertile mind even went so far as to discover that it would prove a blessing to the community, and on this ingenious theory, half honest and half fraudulent, he stretched the widely extended fabric of the web in which all mankind was to be caught. This theory was in itself partially sound. Starting from the principle that the price of grain in New York is regulated by the price in London and is not affected by currency fluctuations, Mr. Gould argued that if it were possible to raise the premium on gold from thirty to forty cents at harvest-time, the farmers' grain would be worth $1.40 instead of $1.30, and as a consequence the farmer would hasten to send all his crop to New York for export, over the Erie Railway, which was sorely in need of freights. With the assistance of another gentleman, Mr. Gould calculated the exact premium at which the Western farmer would consent to dispose of his grain, and thus distance the three hundred sail which were hastening from the Danube to supply the English market. Gold, which was then heavy at 34, must be raised to 45.

This clever idea, like all the other ideas of these gentlemen of Erie, seems to have had the single fault of requiring that some one, somewhere, should be swindled. The scheme was probably feasible; but sooner or later the reaction from such an artificial stimulant must have come, and whenever it came some one must suffer. Nevertheless, Mr. Gould probably argued that so long as the farmer got his money, the Erie Railway its freights, and he himself his small profits on the gold he bought, it was of little consequence who else might be injured; and, indeed, by the time the reaction came, and gold was ready to fall as he expected, Mr. Gould would probably have been ready to assist the process by speculative sales in order to enable the Western farmer to buy his spring goods cheap as he had sold his autumn crops dear. He himself was equally ready to buy gold cheap and sell it dear on his private account; and as he proposed to bleed New York merchants for the benefit of the Western farmer, so he was willing to bleed Broad Street for his own. The patriotic object was, however, the one which for obvious reasons Mr. Gould preferred to put forward most prominently, and on the strength of which he hoped to rest his ambitious structure of intrigue.

In the operation of raising the price of gold from 133 to 145, there was no great difficulty to men who controlled the resources of the Erie Railway. Credit alone was needed, and of credit Mr. Gould had an unlimited supply. The only serious danger lay in the possible action of the national government, which had not taken the same philanthropic view of the public good as was peculiar to the managers of Erie. Secretary Boutwell, who should have assisted Mr. Gould in "bulling" gold, was gravely suspected of being a bear, and of wishing to depress the premiums to nothing. If he were determined to stand in Mr. Gould's path, it was useless even for the combined forces of Erie and Tammany to jostle against him; and it was therefore essential that Mr. Gould should control the government itself, whether by fair means or foul, by persuasion or by purchase. He undertook the task; and now that his proceedings in both directions have been thoroughly drawn into light, it is well worth while for the public to see how dramatic and how artistically admirable a conspiracy in real life may be, when slowly elaborated from the subtle mind of a clever intriguer, and carried into execution by a band of unshrinking scoundrels.

The first requisite for Mr. Gould's purpose was some channel of direct communication with the President; and here he was peculiarly favored by chance. Mr. Abel Rathbone Corbin, formerly lawyer, editor, speculator, lobby-agent, familiar, as he claims, with everything, had succeeded, during his varied career, in accumulating from one or another of his hazardous pursuits a comfortable fortune, and he had crowned his success, at the age of sixty-seven or thereabouts, by contracting a marriage with General Grant's sister, precisely at the moment when General Grant was on the point of reaching the highest eminence possible to an American citizen. To say that Mr. Corbin's moral dignity had passed absolutely pure through the somewhat tainted atmosphere in which his life had been spent, would be flattering him too highly; but at least he was now no longer engaged in any active occupation, and he lived quietly in New York, watching the course of public affairs, and remarkable for an eminent respectability which became the President's brother-in-law. Mr. Gould enjoyed a slight acquaintance with Mr. Corbin, and he proceeded to improve it. He assumed, and he asserts that he really felt, a respect for Mr. Corbin's shrewdness and sagacity. It is amusing to observe that Mr. Corbin claims to have first impressed the famous crop theory on Mr. Gould's mind; while Mr. Gould testifies that he himself indoctrinated Mr. Corbin with this idea, which became a sort of monomania with the President's brother-in-law, who soon began to preach it to the President himself. On the 15th of June, 1869, the President came to New York, and was there the guest of Mr. Corbin, who urged Mr. Gould to call and pay his respects to the Chief Magistrate. Mr. Gould had probably aimed at precisely this result. He called; and the President of the United States not only listened to the president of Erie, but accepted an invitation to Mr. Fisk's theatre, sat in Mr. Fisk's private box, and the next evening became the guest of these two gentlemen on their magnificent Newport steamer, while Mr. Fisk, arrayed, as the newspapers reported, "in a blue uniform, with a broad gilt cap-band, three silver stars on his coat-sleeve, lavender gloves, and a diamond breast-pin as large as a cherry, stood at the gangway, surrounded by his aids, bestarred and bestriped like himself," and welcomed his distinguished friend.

It had been already arranged that the President should on

this occasion be sounded in regard to his financial policy; and when the selected guests—among whom were Mr. Gould, Mr. Fisk, and others—sat down at nine o'clock to supper, the conversation was directed to the subject of finance. "Some one," says Mr. Gould, "asked the President what his view was." The "some one" in question was, of course, Mr. Fisk, who alone had the impudence to put such an inquiry. The President bluntly replied, that there was a certain amount of fictitiousness about the prosperity of the country, and that the bubble might as well be tapped in one way as another. The remark was fatal to Mr. Gould's plans, and he felt it, in his own words, as a wet blanket.

Meanwhile the post of assistant-treasurer at New York had become vacant, and it was a matter of interest to Mr. Gould that some person friendly to himself should occupy this position, which, in its relations to the public, is second in importance only to the secretaryship of the treasury itself. Mr. Gould consulted Mr. Corbin, and Mr. Corbin suggested the name of General Butterfield,—a former officer in the volunteer army. The appointment was not a wise one; nor does it appear in evidence by what means Mr. Corbin succeeded in bringing it about. There is a suggestion that he used Mr. A. T. Stewart, the wealthy importer, as his instrument for the purpose; but whatever the influence may have been, Mr. Corbin appears to have set it in action, and General Butterfield entered upon his duties towards the 1st of July.

The elaborate preparations thus made show that some large scheme was never absent from Mr. Gould's mind, although between the months of May and August he made no attempt to act upon the markets. But between the 20th of August and the 1st of September, in company with Messrs. Woodward and Kimber, two large speculators, he made what is known as a pool, or combination, to raise the premium on gold, and some ten or fifteen millions were bought, but with very little effect on the price. The tendency of the market was downwards, and it was not easily counteracted. Perhaps under ordinary circumstances he might have now abandoned his project; but an incident suddenly occurred which seems to have drawn him headlong into the boldest operations.

Whether the appointment of General Butterfield had any share in strengthening Mr. Gould's faith in Mr. Corbin's secret powers does not appear in evidence, though it may readily be assumed as probable. At all events, an event now took place which would have seemed to authorize an unlimited faith in Mr. Corbin, as well as to justify the implicit belief of an Erie treasurer in the corruptibility of all mankind. The unsuspicious President again passed through New York, and came to breakfast at Mr. Corbin's house on the 2d of September. He saw no one but Mr. Corbin while there, and the same evening at ten o'clock departed for Saratoga. Mr. Gould declares, however, that he was told by Mr. Corbin that the President, in discussing the financial situation, had shown himself a convert to the Erie theory about marketing the crops, and had "stopped in the middle of a conversation in which he had expressed his views, and written a letter" to Secretary Boutwell. This letter is not produced; but Secretary Boutwell testifies as follows in regard to it:—

"I think on the evening of the 4th of September I received a letter from the President dated at New York, as I recollect it; I am not sure where it is dated. I have not seen the letter since the night I received it. I think it is now in my residence in Groton. In that letter he expressed an opinion that it was undesirable to force down the price of gold. He spoke of the importance to the West of being able to move their crops. His idea was that if gold should fall, the West would suffer, and the movement of the crops would be retarded. The impression made on my mind by the letter was that he had rather a strong opinion to that effect. . . . . Upon the receipt of the President's letter on the evening of the 4th of September, I telegraphed to Judge Richardson [Assistant Secretary at Washington] this dispatch: 'Send no order to Butterfield as to sales of gold until you hear from me.' "

Mr. Gould had therefore succeeded in reversing the policy of the national government; but this was not all. He knew what the government would do before any officer of the government knew it. Mr. Gould was at Corbin's house on the 2d of September; and although the evidence of both these gentlemen is very confused on this point, the inference is inevitable that Gould saw Corbin privately, unknown to the President, within an hour or two after this letter to Mr. Boutwell was written, and that it was at this interview, while the President was still in the house, that Mr. Corbin gave him the information about the letter; perhaps showed him the letter itself. Then followed a transaction worthy of the French stage. Mr. Corbin's evidence gives his own account of it:—

"On the 2d of September (referring to memoranda) Mr. Gould offered to let me have some of the gold he then possessed. . . . . He spoke to me as he had repeatedly done before, about taking a certain amount of gold owned by him. I finally told Mr. Gould that for the sake of a lady, my wife, I would accept of $500,000 of gold for her benefit, as I shared his confidence that gold would rise. . . . . He afterwards insisted that I should take a million more, and I did so on the same conditions for my wife. He then sent me this paper."

The paper in question is as follows:—

"Smith, Gould, Martin, & Co., Bankers,
11 Broad Street, New York, September 2, 1869.
"Mr. ——
"Dear Sir: we have bought for your account and risk—
500,000, gold, 132, R.
1,000,000, gold, 133⅝, R.
which we will carry on demand with the right to use.
"SMITH, GOULD, MARTIN, & CO."

This memorandum meant that for every rise of one per cent in the price of gold Mr. Corbin was to receive £3,000, and his name nowhere to appear. If the inference is correct that Gould had seen Corbin in the morning and had learned from him what the President had written, it is clear that he must have made his bargain on the spot, and then going directly to the city, he must in one breath have ordered this memorandum to be made out and large quantities of gold to be purchased, before the President had allowed the letter to leave Mr. Corbin's house.

No time was lost. On this same afternoon, Mr. Gould's brokers bought large amounts in gold. One testifies to buying $1,315,000 at 134⅛. On the 3d the premium was forced up to 36; on the 4th, when Mr. Boutwell received his letter, it had risen to 37. Here, however, Mr. Gould seems to have met a check, and he describes his own position in nervous Americanisms as follows:—

"I did not want to buy so much gold. In the spring I put gold up from 32 to 38 and 40, with only about seven millions. But all these fellows went in and sold short, so that in order to keep it up I had to buy, or else to back down and show the white feather. They would sell it to you all the time. I never intended to buy more than four or five millions of gold, but these fellows kept purchasing it on, and I made up my mind that I would put it up to 40 at one time. . . . . We went into it as a commercial transaction, and did not intend to buy such an amount of gold. I was forced into it by the bears selling out. They were bound to put it down. I got into the contest. All these other fellows deserted me like rats from a ship. Kimber sold out and got short. . . . . He sold out at 37. He got short of it, and went up" (or, in English, he failed).

It was unfortunate that the bears would not consent to lie still and be flayed, but this was unquestionably the fact. They had the great operators for once at a disadvantage, and they were bent on revenge. Mr. Gould's position was very hazardous. When Mr. Kimber sold out at 37, which was probably on the 7th of September, the market broke; and on the 8th the price fell back to 35. Nor was this all. At the same moment, when the "pool" was ended by Mr. Kimber's desertion, Mr. Corbin, with his eminent shrewdness and respectability, told Mr. Gould "that gold had gone up to 37," and that he "should like to have this matter realized," which was equivalent to saying that he wished to be paid something on account. This was on the 6th; and Gould was obliged this same day to bring him a check for £5,000, drawn to the order of Jay Gould, and indorsed in blank by him with a touching regard for Mr.

Corbin's modest desire not to have his name appear. There are few financiers in the world who will not agree that this transaction does great credit to Mr. Corbin's sagacity. It indicates at least that he was acquainted with the men he dealt with. Undoubtedly it placed Mr. Gould in a difficult position; but as Mr. Gould already held some fifteen millions of gold and needed Mr. Corbin's support, he preferred to pay £5,000 outright rather than allow Corbin to throw his gold on the market. Yet the fabric of Gould's web had now been so seriously injured that, for a whole week, from the 8th to the 15th of September, he was at a loss what to do, unable to advance and equally unable to retreat without very severe losses. He sat at his desk in the opera-house, silent as usual, and tearing little slips of paper which he threw on the floor in his abstraction, while he revolved new combinations in his mind.

Down to this moment Mr. James Fisk, Jr., has not appeared in the affair. Gould had not taken him into his confidence; and it was not until after the 10th of September that Gould appears to have decided that there was nothing else to be done. Fisk was not a safe ally in so delicate an affair, but apparently there was no choice. Gould approached him; and, as usual, his touch was like magic. Mr. Fisk's evidence begins here, and may be believed when very strongly corroborated:

"Gold having settled down to 35, and I not having cared to touch it, he was a little sensitive on the subject, feeling as if he would rather take his losses without saying anything about it. . . . . One day he said to me, 'Don't you think gold has got to the bottom?' I replied that I did not see the profit in buying gold unless you have got into a position where you can command the market. He then said he had bought quite a large amount of gold, and I judged from his conversation that he wanted me to go into the movement and help strengthen the market. Upon that I went into the market and bought. I should say that was about the 15th or 16th of September. I bought at that time about seven or eight millions, I think."

The market responded slowly to these enormous purchases; and on the 16th the clique was still struggling to recover its lost ground.

Meanwhile Mr. Gould had placed another million and a half of gold to the account of General Butterfield, and notified him of the purchase. So Mr. Gould swears in spite of General Butterfield's denial. The date of this purchase is not fixed. Through Mr. Corbin a notice was also sent by Gould about the middle of September to the President's private secretary, General Porter, informing him that half a million was placed to his credit. General Porter instantly wrote to repudiate the purchase, but it does not appear that Butterfield took any notice of Gould's transaction on his account. On the 10th of September the President had again come to New York, where he remained his brother-in-law's guest till the 13th; and during this visit Mr. Gould appears again to have seen him, although Mr. Corbin avers that on this occasion the President intimated his wish to the servant that this should be the last time Mr. Gould obtained admission. "Gould was always trying to get something out of him," he said; and if he had known how much Mr. Gould had succeeded in getting out of him, he would have admired the man's genius, even while shutting the door in his face. On the morning of the 13th the President set out on a journey to the little town of Washington, situated among the mountains of Western Pennsylvania, where he was to remain a few days. Mr. Gould, who now consulted Mr. Corbin regularly every morning and evening, was still extremely nervous in regard to the President's policy; and as the crisis approached, this nervousness led him into the fatal blunder of doing too much. The bribe offered to Porter was a grave mistake, but a greater mistake yet was made by pressing Mr. Corbin's influence too far. He induced Mr. Corbin to write an official article for the New York press on the financial policy of the government, an article afterwards inserted in the New York Times through the kind offices of Mr. James McHenry, and he also persuaded or encouraged Mr. Corbin to write a letter directly to the President himself. This letter, written on the 17th under the influence of Gould's anxiety, was instantly sent away by a special messenger of Fisk's to reach the President before he returned to the capital.

The messenger carried also a letter of introduction to General Porter, the private secretary, in order to secure the personal delivery of this important despatch.

We have now come to the week which was to witness the explosion of all this elaborately constructed mine. On Monday, the 20th, gold again rose. Throughout Tuesday and Wednesday Fisk continued to purchase without limit, and forced the price up to 40. At this time Gould's firm of Smith, Gould, & Martin, through which the operation was conducted, had purchased some $50,000,000; and yet the bears went on selling, although they could only continue the contest by borrowing Gould's own gold. Gould, on the other hand, could no longer sell and clear himself, for the very reason that the sale of $50,000,000 would have broken the market to nothing. The struggle had become intense. The whole country was looking on with astonishment at the battle between the bulls and the bears. All business was deranged, and all values unsettled. There were indications of a panic in the stock market; and the bears in their emergency were vehemently pressing the government to intervene. Gould now wrote to Mr. Boutwell a letter so inconceivably impudent that it indicates desperation and entire loss of his ordinary coolness. He began:—

"SIR,—There is a panic in Wall Street, engineered by a bear combination. They have withdrawn currency to such an extent that it is impossible to do ordinary business. The Erie Company requires eight hundred thousand dollars to disburse. . . . . Much of it in Ohio, where an exciting political contest is going on, and where we have about ten thousand employed, and the trouble is charged on the administration. . . . . Cannot you, consistently, increase your line of currency?"

From a friend such a letter would have been an outrage; but from a member of the Tammany ring, the principal object of detestation to the government, such a threat or bribe— whichever it may be called—was incredible. Mr. Gould was, in fact, at his wits' end. He dreaded a panic, and he felt that it could no longer be avoided.

The scene now shifts for a moment to the distant town of Washington, among the hills of Western Pennsylvania. On the morning of the 19th of September, President Grant and his private secretary, General Porter, were playing croquet on the grass, when Fisk's messenger, after twenty-four hours of travel by rail and carriage, arrived at the house, and sent in to ask for General Porter. When the President's game was ended, General Porter came, received his own letter from Corbin, and called the President, who entered the room and took his brother-in-law's despatch. He then left the room, and after some ten or fifteen minutes' absence returned. The messenger, tired of waiting, then asked, "Is it all right?" "All right," replied the President; and the messenger hastened to the nearest telegraph station, and sent word to Fisk, "Delivered; all right."

The messenger was, however, altogether mistaken. Not only was all not right, but all was going hopelessly wrong. The President, it appears, had at the outset supposed the man to be an ordinary post-office agent, and the letter an ordinary letter which had arrived through the post-office. Nor was it until Porter asked some curious question as to the man, that the President learned of his having been sent by Corbin merely to carry this apparently unimportant letter of advice. The President's suspicions were at once excited; and the same evening, at his request, Mrs. Grant wrote a hurried note to Mrs. Corbin, telling her how greatly the President was distressed at the rumor that Mr. Corbin was speculating in Wall Street, and how much he hoped that Mr. Corbin would "instantly disconnect himself with anything of that sort."

This letter, subsequently destroyed or said to have been destroyed by Mrs. Corbin, arrived in New York on the morning of Wednesday the 22d, the same day on which Gould and his enemies the bears were making their simultaneous appeals to Secretary Boutwell. Mrs. Corbin was greatly excited and distressed by her sister-in-law's language. She at once carried the letter to her husband, and insisted that he should instantly abandon his interest in the gold speculation. Mr. Corbin, although he considered the scruples of his wife and her family to be highly absurd, assented to her wish; and when Mr. Gould came that evening as usual, with $50,000,000 of gold on his hands, and extreme anxiety on his mind, Corbin read to him two letters: the first, written by Mrs. Grant to Mrs. Corbin; the second, written by Mr. Corbin to President Grant, assuring him that he had not a dollar of interest in gold. The assurance of this second letter was, at any sacrifice, to be made good.

Mr. Corbin proposed that Mr. Gould should give him a check for £20,000, and take his $1,500,000 off his hands. A proposition more calmly impudent than this can scarcely be imagined. Gould had already paid Corbin £5,000, and Corbin asked for £20,000 more, at the very moment when it was clear that the £5,000 he had received had been given him under a misunderstanding of his services. He even had the impudence to represent himself as doing Gould a favor by letting him have a million and a half more gold at the highest market price, at a time when Gould had fifty millions which it was clear he must sell or be ruined. What Gould might, under ordinary circumstances, have replied, may be imagined; but at this moment he could say nothing. Corbin had but to show this note to a single broker in Wall Street, and the whole fabric of Gould's speculation would have fallen to pieces. Gould asked for time and went away. He consulted no one. He gave Fisk no hint of what had happened. The next morning he returned to Corbin, and made him the following offer:—

" 'Mr. Corbin, I cannot give you anything if you will go out. If you will remain in, and take the chances of the market, I will give you my check [for £20,000].' 'And then,' says Mr. Corbin, 'I did what I think it would have troubled almost any other business man to consent to do,—refuse one hundred thousand dollars on a rising market. If I had not been an old man married to a middle-aged woman, I should have done it (of course with her consent) just as sure as the offer was made. I said, 'Mr. Gould, my wife says "No!" Ulysses thinks it wrong, and that it ought to end.' So

I gave it up. . . . . He looked at me with an air of severe distrust, as if he was afraid of treachery in the camp. He remarked, 'Mr. Corbin, I am undone if that letter gets out.' . . . . He stood there for a little while looking very thoughtful, exceedingly thoughtful. He then left and went into Wall Street, ... and my impression is that he it was, and not the government, that broke that market.' "

Mr. Corbin was right; throughout all these transactions his insight into Mr. Gould's character was marvellous.

It was the morning of Thursday, the 3d; Gould and Fisk went to Broad Street together, but as usual Gould was silent and secret, while Fisk was noisy and communicative. There was now a complete separation in their movements. Gould acted entirely through his own firm of Smith, Gould, & Martin, while Fisk operated principally through his old partner, Belden. One of Smith's principal brokers testifies:—

" 'Fisk never could do business with Smith, Gould, & Martin very comfortably. They would not do business for him. It was a very uncertain thing of course where Fisk might be. He is an erratic sort of genius. I don't think anybody would want to follow him very long. I am satisfied that Smith, Gould, & Martin controlled their own gold, and were ready to do as they pleased with it without consulting Fisk. I do not think there was any general agreement. . . . . None of us who knew him cared to do business with him. I would not have taken an order from him nor had anything to do with him.' Belden was considered a very low fellow. 'I never had anything to do with him or his party,' said one broker employed by Gould. 'They were men I had a perfect detestation of; they were no company for me. I should not have spoken to them at all under any ordinary circumstances.' Another says, 'Belden is a man in whom I never had any confidence in any way. For months before that, I would not have taken him for a gold transaction.' "

And yet Belden bought millions upon millions of gold. He himself says he had bought twenty millions by this Thursday evening, and this without capital or credit except that of his brokers. Meanwhile Gould, on reaching the city, had at once given secret orders to sell. From the moment he left Corbin, he had but one idea, which was to get rid of his gold as quietly as possible. "I purchased merely enough to make believe I was a bull," says Gould. This double process continued all that afternoon. Fisk's wild purchases carried the price up to 144, and the panic in the street became more and more serious as the bears realized the extremity of their danger. No one can tell how much gold which did not exist they had contracted to deliver or pay the difference in price. One of the clique brokers swears that on this Thursday evening the street had sold the clique one hundred and eighteen millions of gold, and every rise of one per cent on this sum implied a loss of more than £200,000 to the bears. Naturally the terror was extreme, for half Broad Street and thousands of speculators would have been ruined if compelled to settle gold at 150 which they had sold at 140. It need scarcely be said that by this time nothing more was heard in regard to philanthropic theories of benefit to the Western farmer.

Mr. Gould's feelings can easily be imagined. He knew that Fisk's reckless management would bring the government upon his shoulders, and he knew that unless he could sell his gold before the order came from Washington he would be a ruined man. He knew, too, that Fisk's contracts must inevitably be repudiated. This Thursday evening he sat at his desk in the Erie offices at the opera-house, while Fisk and Fisk's brokers chattered about him.

"I was transacting my railway business. I had my own views about the market, and my own fish to fry. I was all alone, so to speak, in what I did, and I did not let any of those people know exactly how I stood. I got no ideas from anything that was said there. I had been selling gold from 35 up all the time, and I did not know till the next morning that there would probably come an order about twelve o'clock to sell gold."

He had not told Fisk a word in regard to Corbin's retreat, nor his own orders to sell.

When the next day came, Gould and Fisk went together to Broad Street, and took possession of the private back office of a principal broker, "without asking the privilege of doing so," as the broker observes in his evidence. The first news brought to Gould was a disaster. The government had sent three men from Washington to examine the bank which Gould owned, and the bank sent word to Mr. Gould that it feared to certify for him as usual, and was itself in danger of a panic, caused by the presence of officers, which created distrust of the bank. It barely managed to save itself. Gould took the information silently, and his firm redoubled sales of gold. His partner, Smith, gave the orders to one broker after another,—"Sell ten millions!" "The order was given as quick as a flash, and away he went," says one of these men. "I sold only eight millions." "Sell, sell, sell! do nothing but sell!—only don't sell to Fisk's brokers," were the orders which Smith himself acknowledges. In the gold-room Fisk's brokers were shouting their rising bids, and the packed crowd grew frantic with terror and rage as each successive rise showed their increasing losses. The wide streets outside were thronged with excited people; the telegraph offices were overwhelmed with messages ordering sales or purchases of gold or stocks; and the whole nation was watching eagerly to see what the result of this convulsion was to be. All trade was stopped, and even the President felt that it was time to raise his hand. No one who has not seen the New York gold-room can understand the spectacle it presented; now a perfect pandemonium, now silent as the grave. Fisk, in his dark back office across the street, with his coat off, swaggered up and down, "a big cane in his hand," and called himself the Napoleon of Wall Street. He really believed that he directed the movement, and while the street outside imagined that he and Gould were one family, and that his purchases were made for the clique, Gould was silently flinging away his gold at any price he could get for it.

Whether Fisk really expected to carry out his contract, and force the bears to settle, or not, is doubtful; but the evidence seems to show that he was in earnest, and felt sure of success. His orders were unlimited. "Put it up to 150," was one which he sent to the gold-room. Gold rose to 150. At length the bid was made—"160 for any part of five millions," and

no one any longer dared take it. "161 for five millions,"—
"162 for five millions." No answer was made, and the offer
was repeated,—"162 for any part of five millions." A voice
replied, "Sold one million at 62." The bubble suddenly
burst, and within fifteen minutes, amid an excitement without
parallel even in the wildest excitements of the war, the clique
brokers were literally swept away, and left struggling by themselves, bidding still 160 for gold in millions which no one
would any longer take their word for; while the premium sank
rapidly to 135. A moment later the telegraph brought from
Washington the government order to sell, and the result was
no longer possible to dispute. Mr. Fisk had gone too far, while
Mr. Gould had secretly weakened the ground under his feet.

Gould, however, was saved. His fifty millions were sold;
and although no one yet knows what his gains or losses may
have been, his firm was now able to meet its contracts and
protect its brokers. Fisk was in a very different situation.
So soon as it became evident that his brokers would be unable
to carry out their contracts, every one who had sold gold to
them turned in wrath to Fisk's office. Fortunately for him
it was protected by armed men whom he had brought with
him from his castle of Erie; but nevertheless the excitement
was so great that both Mr. Fisk and Mr. Gould thought it best
to retire as rapidly as possible by a back entrance leading into
another street, and to seek the protection of the opera-house.
There nothing but an army could disturb them; no civil man-
date was likely to be served without their permission within
these walls, and few men would care to face Fisk's ruffians in
order to force an entrance.

The subsequent winding up of this famous conspiracy may
be stated in few words. But no account could possibly be
complete which failed to reproduce in full the story of Mr.
Fisk's last interview with Mr. Corbin, as told by Fisk himself.

"I went down to the neighborhood of Wall Street, Friday morning, and the history of that morning you know. When I got back
to our office, you can imagine I was in no enviable state of mind,

and the moment I got up street that afternoon I started right round to old Corbin's to rake him out. I went into the room, and sent word that Mr. Fisk wanted to see him in the dining-room. I was too mad to say anything civil, and when he came into the room, said I, 'You damned old scoundrel, do you know what you have done here, you and your people?' He began to wring his hands, and, 'Oh!' he says, 'this is a horrible position. Are you ruined?' I said I didn't know whether I was or not; and I asked him again if he knew what had happened? He had been crying, and said he had just heard; that he had been sure everything was all right; but that something had occurred entirely different from what he had anticipated. Said I, 'That don't amount to anything; we know that gold ought not to be at 31, and that it would not be but for such performances as you have had this last week; you know damned well it would not if you had not failed.' I knew that somebody had run a saw right into us, and said I, 'This whole damned thing has turned out just as I told you it would.' I considered the whole party a pack of cowards, and I expected that when we came to clear our hands they would sock it right into us. I said to him, 'I don't know whether you have lied or not, and I don't know what ought to be done with you.' He was on the other side of the table, weeping and wailing, and I was gnashing my teeth. 'Now,' he says, 'you must quiet yourself.' I told him I didn't want to be quiet. I had no desire to ever be quiet again, and probably never should be quiet again. He says, 'But, my dear sir, you will lose your reason.' Says I, 'Speyers [a broker employed by him that day] has already lost his reason; reason has gone out of everybody but me.' I continued, 'Now what are you going to do? You have got us into this thing, and what are you going to do to get out of it?' He says, 'I don't know. I will go and get my wife.' I said, 'Get her down here!' The soft talk was all over. He went up stairs and they returned, tottling into the room, looking older than Stephen Hopkins. His wife and he both looked like death. He was tottling just like that. [Illustrated by a trembling movement of his body.] I have never seen him from that day to this."

This is sworn evidence before a committee of Congress; and its humor is perhaps the more conspicuous, because there is every reason to believe that there is not a word of truth in the story from beginning to end. No such interview ever occurred, except in the unconfined apartments of Mr. Fisk's imagination. His own previous statements make it certain that he was not at Corbin's house at all that day, and that Corbin did come to the Erie offices that evening, and again the next morning. Corbin himself denies the truth of the account without limitation; and adds, that when he entered the Erie offices the next morning Fisk was there. "I asked him how Mr. Gould felt after the great calamity of the day before." He remarked, "O, he has no courage at all. He has sunk right down. There is nothing left of him but a heap of clothes and a pair of eyes." The internal evidence of truth in this anecdote would support Mr. Corbin against the world.[3]

[3] Mr. Fisk to the Editor of the Sun:—

Erie Railway Company, Comptroller's Office,

NEW YORK, October 4, 1869.

TO THE EDITOR OF THE SUN.

Dear Sir,—. . . . Mr. Corbin has constantly associated with me; . . . . *he spent more than an hour with me in the Erie Railway Office on the afternoon of Saturday, September 25th, the day after the gold panic.* . . . . I enclose you a few affidavits which will give you further information concerning this matter.

I remain your obedient servant,

JAMES FISK, JR.

Affidavit of Charles W. Pollard.

"State of New York, City and County of New York, ss.

"C. W. Pollard, being duly sworn, says: 'I have frequently been the bearer of messages between Mr. James Fisk, Jr., and Mr. Abel R. Corbin, brother-in-law of President Grant. . . . . Mr. Corbin called on me at the Erie building on Thursday, 23d September, 1869, telling me he came to see how Messrs. Fisk and Gould were getting along. . . . . He called again on Friday, the following day, at about noon; appeared to be greatly excited and said he feared *we* should lose a great deal of money. The following morning, Saturday, September 25, Mr. Fisk told me to take his carriage and call upon Mr. Corbin and say to him that he and Mr. Gould would like to see him (Corbin) at their office. I called and saw Mr. Corbin. He remarked upon greeting me: "How does Mr. Fisk bear his losses?" and added, *"It is terrible for us."* He then asked me to bring Mr. Fisk up to his house immediately, as he was indisposed, and did not feel able to go down to his (Fisk's) office. I went after Mr. Fisk, who returned immediately with me to Mr. Corbin's residence, but shortly after came out with Mr. Corbin, who accompanied him to Mr. Fisk's office,

In regard to Mr. Gould, Fisk's graphic description was probably again inaccurate. Undoubtedly the noise and scandal of the moment were extremely unpleasant to this silent and impenetrable intriguer. The city was in a ferment, and the whole country pointing at him with wrath. The machinery of the gold exchange had broken down, and he alone could extricate the business community from the pressing danger of a general panic. He had saved himself, it is true; but in a manner which could not have been to his taste. Yet his course from this point must have been almost self-evident to his mind, and there is no reason to suppose that he hesitated.

His own contracts were all fulfilled. Fisk's contracts, all except one, in respect to which the broker was able to compel a settlement, were repudiated. Gould probably suggested to Fisk that it was better to let Belden fail, and to settle a handsome fortune on him, than to sacrifice something more than £1,000,000 in sustaining him. Fisk therefore threw Belden over, and swore that he had acted only under Belden's order; in support of which statement he produced a paper to the following effect:—

"September 24.

"DEAR SIR,—I hereby authorize you to order the purchase and sale of gold on my account during this day to the extent you may deem advisable, and to report the same to me as early as possible. It is to be understood that the profits of such order are to belong entirely to me, and I will, of course, bear any losses resulting.

"Yours,

"WILLIAM BELDEN.

"JAMES FISK, JR."

This document was not produced in the original, and certainly never existed. Belden himself could not be induced to

---

where he was closeted with him and Mr. Gould for about two hours. . . . .'"

There are obvious inconsistencies among these different accounts, which it is useless to attempt to explain. The fact of Saturday's interview appears, however, to be beyond dispute.

acknowledge the order; and no one would have believed him if he had done so. Meanwhile the matter is before the national courts, and Fisk may probably be held to his contracts: but it will be far more difficult to execute judgment upon him, or to discover his assets.

One of the first acts of the Erie gentlemen after the crisis was to summon their lawyers, and set in action their judicial powers. The object was to prevent the panic-stricken brokers from using legal process to force settlements, and so render the entanglement inextricable. Messrs. Field and Shearman came, and instantly prepared a considerable number of injunctions, which were sent to their judges, signed at once, and immediately served. Gould then was able to dictate the terms of settlement; and after a week of complete paralysis, Broad Street began at last to show signs of returning life. As a legal curiosity, one of these documents, issued three months after the crisis, may be reproduced, in order to show the powers wielded by the Erie managers:—

"SUPREME COURT.

H. N. SMITH, JAY GOULD, H. H. MARTIN, and J. B. BACH, Plaintiffs,
against
JOHN BONNER and ARTHUR L. SEWELL, Defendants,

Injunction by order.

"It appearing satisfactorily to me by the complaint duly verified by the plaintiffs that sufficient grounds for an order of injunction exist, I do hereby order and enjoin . . . . That the defendants, John Bonner and Arthur L. Sewell, their agents, attorneys, and servants, refrain from pressing their pretended claims against the plaintiffs, or either of them, before the Arbitration Committee of the New York Stock Exchange, or from taking any proceedings thereon, or in relation thereto, except in this action.

"GEORGE G. BARNARD, J. S. C.

"NEW YORK, December 29, 1869."

Mr. Bonner had practically been robbed with violence by Mr. Gould, and instead of his being able to bring the robber into court as the criminal, the robber brought him into court as criminal, and the judge forbade him to appear in any other character. Of all Mr. Field's distinguished legal reforms and philanthropic projects, this injunction is beyond a doubt the most brilliant and the most successful.[4]

[4] These remarks on Mr. Field's professional conduct as counsel of the Erie Railway have excited a somewhat intemperate controversy, and Mr. Field's partisans in the press have made against the authors of the "Chapters of Erie" a charge which certainly has the merit of even exaggerated modesty on the part of the New York bench and bar, namely, that these writers "have indelicately interfered in a matter alien to them in every way"; the administration of justice in New York being, in this point of view, a matter in which Mr. Field and the Erie Railway are alone concerned. Mr. Field himself has published a letter in the Westminster Review for April, 1871, in which, after the general assertion that the passages in the "New York Gold Conspiracy" which relate to him "cover about as much untruth as could be crowded into so many lines," he proceeds to make the following corrections:

First, he denies, what was never suggested, that he was in any way a party to the origin or progress of the Gold Conspiracy; until (secondly) he was consulted on the 28th of September; when (thirdly) he gave an opinion as to the powers of the members of the Gold and Stock Exchanges. Fourthly, he denies that he has relations of any sort with any judge in New York, or any power over these judges, other than such as English counsel have in respect to English judges. Fifthly, he asserts that out of twenty-eight injunctions growing out of the gold transactions, his partners obtained only ten, and only one of these ten, the one quoted above, from Justice Barnard. Sixthly, that this injunction was proper to be sought and granted. Seventhly, that Mr. Bonner was not himself the person who had been "robbed with violence," but the assignee of the parties.

On the other hand it does not appear that Mr. Field denies that the injunction as quoted is genuine, or that he is responsible for it, or that it did, as asserted, shut the defendants out of the courts as well as out of the Gold Exchange Arbitration Committee, or that it compelled them to appear only as defendants in a case where they were the injured parties.

In regard to the power which Mr. Field, whether as a private individual or as Erie counsel, has exercised over the New York bench, his modest denial is hardly calculated to serve as a final answer. And in regard to Mr. Bonner, the fact of his being principal or representative scarcely affects the character of Mr. Field's injunction. Finally, so far as the text is concerned, after allowing full weight to all Mr. Field's corrections, the public can decide for itself how many untruths it contains. The subject

The fate of the conspirators was not severe. Mr. Corbin went to Washington, where he was snubbed by the President, and at once disappeared from public view, only coming to light again before the Congressional Committee. General Butterfield, whose share in the transaction is least understood, was permitted to resign his office without an investigation. Speculation for the next six months was at an end. Every person involved in the affair seemed to have lost money, and dozens of brokers were swept from the street. But Mr. Jay Gould and Mr. James Fisk, Jr., continued to reign over Erie, and no one can say that their power or their credit was sensibly diminished by a shock which for the time prostrated all the interests of the country.

Nevertheless it is safe to predict that sooner or later the last traces of the disturbing influence of war and paper money will disappear in America, as they have sooner or later disappeared in every other country which has passed through the same evils. The result of this convulsion itself has been in the main good. It indicates the approaching end of a troubled time. Messrs. Gould and Fisk will at last be obliged to yield to the force of moral and economical laws. The Erie Railway will be rescued, and its history will perhaps rival that of the great speculative manias of the last century. The United States will restore a sound basis to its currency, and will learn to deal with the political reforms it requires. Yet though the regular process of development may be depended upon, in its ordinary and established course, to purge American society of the worst agents of an exceptionally corrupt time, there is in the history of this Erie corporation one matter in regard to which modern society everywhere is directly interested. For the first time since the creation of these enormous corporate

---

has, however, ceased to be one of consequence even to Mr. Field since the subsequent violent controversy which arose in March, 1871, in regard to other points of Mr. Field's professional conduct, and in another month after his letter was written he would perhaps have thought the comments of the Westminster Review so comparatively trifling in importance as not to deserve his attention.

bodies, one of them has shown its power for mischief, and has proved itself able to override and trample on law, custom, decency, and every restraint known to society, without scruple, and as yet without check. The belief is common in America that the day is at hand when corporations far greater than the Erie—swaying power such as has never in the world's history been trusted in the hands of mere private citizens, controlled by single men like Vanderbilt, or by combinations of men like Fisk, Gould, and Lane, after having created a system of quiet but irresistible corruption—will ultimately succeed in directing government itself. Under the American form of society, there is now no authority capable of effective resistance. The national government, in order to deal with the corporations, must assume powers refused to it by its fundamental law, and even then is always exposed to the chance of forming an absolute central government which sooner or later is likely to fall into the very hands it is struggling to escape, and thus destroy the limits of its power only in order to make corruption omnipotent. Nor is this danger confined to America alone. The corporation is in its nature a threat against the popular institutions which are spreading so rapidly over the whole world. Wherever there is a popular and limited government this difficulty will be found in its path, and unless some satisfactory solution of the problem can be reached, popular institutions may yet find their very existence endangered.

An Erie Raid

HISTORY scarcely affords a parallel to the rapid development of character which took place in America during the five years of the late civil war. At its close the ordinary results of long internal strife were conspicuous only by their absence. No chronic guerilla warfare was sustained in the South, and in the North no unusual license or increase of crime revealed the presence of a million of men unaccustomed to habits of industry and inured to a life of arms. Yet while these superficial indications of change would be sought in vain, other and far more suggestive phases of development cannot but force themselves on the attention of any thoughtful observer. The most noticeable of these is perhaps to be found in a greatly enlarged grasp of enterprise and increased facility of combination. The great operations of war, the handling of large masses of men, the influence of discipline, the lavish expenditure of unprecedented sums of money, the immense financial operations, the possibilities of effective co-operation, were lessons not likely to be lost on men quick to receive and to apply all new ideas. Those keen observers who looked for strange and unexpected phenomena when the struggle in the field was over have indeed witnessed that which must have surpassed all anticipation.

If the five years that succeeded the war have been marked by no exceptional criminal activity, they have witnessed some of the most remarkable examples of organized lawlessness, under the forms of law, which mankind has yet had an opportunity to study. If individuals have, as a rule, quietly pursued their peaceful vocations, the same cannot be said of certain single men at the head of vast combinations of private wealth. This has been peculiarly the case as regards those controlling the rapidly developed railroad interests. These modern potentates have declared war, negotiated peace, reduced courts, legislatures, and sovereign States to an unqualified obedience to their will, disturbed trade, agitated the currency, imposed taxes, and, boldly setting both law and public opinion at defiance, have freely exercised many other attributes of sovereignty. Neither have the means at disposal proved at all inadequate to the ends in view. Single men have controlled hundreds of miles of railway, thousands of men, tens of millions of revenue, and hundreds of millions of capital. The strength implied in all this they wielded in practical independence of the control both of governments and of individuals; much as petty German despots might have governed their little principalities a century or two ago. Thus by degrees almost the whole of the system of internal communication through the northern half of the United States has practically been partitioned out among a few individuals, and, as proximity, or competition on certain debatable grounds,—the Belgiums of the system,—brought the interests represented by these men into conflict, a series of struggles have ensued replete with dramatic episodes. No history of the present time will be complete in which these do not occupy much space, and any condensed record of them has, therefore, much more than a passing value. Not history in itself, it contains the material of history; yet the thread of these episodes is so difficult to trace, lying concealed in such dull volumes of evidence and records of the law, or preserved only in the knowledge of individuals, that unless it be found at once it is in danger of being lost forever. The speedy oblivion which covers up events that, for a time, fasten public attention and seem big with great results, is indeed one of the noticeable indications of the times. The practical experience of this fact has tended greatly to encourage all sorts of violations both of law and of morals. There seems no longer to be any Nemesis to dog the evil-doer. Men are to-day in all mouths infamous from active participation in some great scandal or fraud,—some stock operation or gambler's conspiracy, some gold combination or Erie Railway war, some Credit Mobilier's contractor's job or Hartford & Erie scandal, —and to-morrow a new outrage, in another quarter, works a sudden condonation of each offence.

Nothing could more fully illustrate the rapidity with which such episodes as those referred to are forgotten than the complete oblivion into which the struggle in 1869 for the possession of the Albany & Susquehanna Railroad has fallen. This contest, marked by legal scandals almost unparalleled, and actually resulting in an attempt at armed warfare between corporations, though not yet finally passed upon by the courts, is fairly forgotten by the world. It was, however, not without elements of a permanent interest, though no consecutive account of it has yet been attempted. The following narrative, drawn almost exclusively from the sworn evidence and official records in the case, probably presents the story with as near an approach to accuracy as is now likely ever to be arrived at.

The business of transportation by rail naturally divides itself into the two great elements of through and local traffic. The Erie Railway was especially constructed with a view to through traffic, and the New York Central, though originally consisting in a chain of disconnected local roads, through the force of circumstances and by a natural process of development, early became one of the great trunk lines of the continent. The Albany & Susquehanna, on the contrary, was designed by its projectors as a purely local road. As such its history could never have been a very interesting one, except to its projectors and owners. It happened, however, to occupy a bit of debatable territory between the two great trunk lines just mentioned, and hence derived its importance. New England has always been in railroad history a sort of an appanage of the Central Railroad of New York. Both freight and passengers passing to and fro between Boston and the West naturally took Albany on their way, and the Central Road, monopolizing as it did the one natural gap in the mountain ranges which divided the interior basin from the sea, looked upon this traffic as its inalienable property. The Albany & Susquehanna Railroad started from this eastern terminus of the Central, and was intended to open it to the Erie at the city of Binghamton, some one hundred and forty miles from the point of departure. In the early days of the enterprise through traffic was less regarded by railroad managers than it now is, and the future significance of this link in their system was hardly realized by either of the great trunk lines. The carriage of freight was then but little understood, and grades were of far greater importance than they now are. Valley roads, it was supposed, might safely ignore the mountain track. This the Albany & Susquehanna certainly was. The region through which it passes is very broken, though it ranks among the finest of the agricultural districts of New York. Starting from that point where the great Alleghany range gradually sinks away into the valley of the Mohawk, the road skirts the base of the heights of Helderberg, an outlying spur of the Catskills, famous once as the seat of the anti-rent troubles, and then, passing among the large rolling hills of Southeastern New York, it gradually climbs the watershed. The route was a difficult one, and the road was costly of construction; laid out on the broad-gauge principle, as a contemplated feeder of the Erie, it was forced to scale ridge after ridge in working its way from one picturesque valley to another, through which to find a natural roadway to its destination. The country along the line is of a hilly rather than a mountainous character, partaking more of the appearance of Vermont than of New Hampshire; timbered lands and cultivated fields alternate over the loftiest summits, and there is something peculiarly attractive in the primitive nestling appearance of the towns and villages. The road thus was projected through a difficult and sequestered region, neither wealthy nor of varied industries, opening to a new trade neither great markets nor a peculiarly active people. It encountered, therefore, even more than the average amount of those financial tribulations which mark the early history of all railroads.

The company was organized in 1852, and the work of construction was begun in 1853, with one million dollars raised by individual subscription along the line of the road; further sums in aid of construction were subsequently received from the towns likely to be benefited by the line, which, by an act of special legislation, were authorized to subscribe to its stock; a loan of one million dollars was likewise obtained from the city of Albany, upon a pledge of the first-mortgage bonds of the company. The process of construction was, however, very slow. The work begun in 1853 was suspended in 1854 on account of the failure of the contractors; it was recommenced in 1857, and then slowly dragged along to completion, a very contractors' Golgotha. Eight times did acts extending to it the financial aid of the State pass the legislature; but they were encountered by six Executive vetoes, and from this source the company realized but seven hundred and fifty thousand dollars. That the scheme was successfully carried out at all was mainly due to the good pluck and untiring industry of one man, Joseph H. Ramsey,—at once the originator, president, financial agent, legal adviser, and guiding spirit of the enterprise.

The close of the seventeenth year of corporate life found all the available means of the company exhausted, and every one connected with it, except Mr. Ramsey, thoroughly discouraged and despondent, with the twenty-two last and most difficult miles of the work yet unfinished. In this emergency the company once more looked to the State for assistance. Through the management of Mr. Ramsey, who had himself in former times more than once assumed the duties of a State legislator in behalf of the enterprise, the necessary act was passed. Most unexpectedly it encountered a veto, the sixth of the series. With an empty treasury, with heavy payments to contractors and on account of interest already due, and with other similar payments rapidly maturing,—with bankruptcy staring him in the face, and with all sources of supply apparently exhausted,—under all these disheartening aspects of the case Mr. Ramsey did not despair. The company had in its safe two classes of securities and two only on which the further necessary loans could possibly be effected. It had a portion of its own second-mortgage bonds and some nine thousand shares of its capital stock, on which various instalments ranging from ten to forty per cent had been paid by the original subscribers. This stock and the subscriptions upon it had subsequently been declared forfeited by a vote of the Board of Directors, with the consent of the holders, for the non-payment of the balance of subscriptions. A law of New York prescribed that no railroad should issue its stock for less than its par value. This law, however, the courts had held did not apply to forfeited stock in the treasury of the company. The difficulty in the case was not in putting the stock on the market, but in finding a purchaser for it when it got there; it had no market price; as an investment it ranked far from high, and, unlike the Erie, it had at this time no value for "speculative purposes." Under these circumstances it seemed possible to the directors to make this one of their two securities available only as a make-weight,—a *douceur,* it might be said, to the other. Two loans were effected accordingly, under a resolution which received the unanimous approval of the Board of Directors on the 3d of June, 1868. The first was with Azro Chase, who became the purchaser of fifty thousand dollars of the second-mortgage bonds at seventy per cent of their par value, with the additional right or option of taking at any time three hundred shares of the forfeited stock at twenty dollars per share. This loan was negotiated through one of the directors of the company named

Leonard, acting as its financial agent, and amounted to the sale of eighty thousand dollars, in the nominal securities of the company, for the sum of forty-one thousand dollars in cash. Two hundred shares of the stock, as it afterwards appeared, passed into the pockets of the director and financial agent as a species of brokerage commission. The second loan was negotiated by Mr. Ramsey himself with Mr. David Groesbeck, the head of a well-known brokers' firm in the city of New York, and formerly the business associate of Mr. Daniel Drew. This loan was upon terms somewhat more favorable to the company than the other, and there were no indications of brokerage in the case. The company received five hundred and sixty thousand dollars, and pledged as collateral its second-mortgage bonds at seventy per cent, with the privilege of purchasing them at any time within eighteen months at eighty, and a similar privilege as regarded twenty-four hundred shares of the forfeited stock at twenty-five dollars per share. In other words, if the lenders availed themselves of the option, as they subsequently did, securities to the nominal value of one million and forty thousand dollars were sold to them for seven hundred thousand dollars in cash. This must certainly be considered as a very advantageous bargain for the company; thirty per cent is a large profit, but it here represented a very unusual risk. Both of these loans received the unanimous sanction of the Board of Directors, and that to Groesbeck played a most important part in the subsequent struggle for the possession of the road.

With the money thus raised the enterprise was at last carried through, and, on the 15th of January, 1869, seventeen years after the organization of the company, the cities of Binghamton and Albany were brought into direct communication. Meanwhile those seventeen years of construction had greatly altered all the conditions of that railroad system of which the Albany & Susquehanna Railroad was now for the first time to become an integral part. In 1853 both the Erie and the Central were but feebly entering on their great careers. The Erie was just completed to Dunkirk: the Central was not yet consolidated; the whole receipts of the first were but one third part of what the completion of Mr. Ramsey's road found them, while, during the same interval, the receipts of the last had swollen from less than six millions per annum to considerably over fifteen. As for the men who managed the great trunk lines when Mr. Ramsey had completed his work, their names had never been mentioned in connection with railroads when he began it. In fact, the whole aspect of the problem had changed. In 1853 all the roads in the country were local roads; in 1869 no local road was suffered to exist, unless the great through roads were satisfied that it could serve no purpose in their hands; nay, more, unless they were also satisfied that it could serve no purpose in the hands of their competitors. When, therefore, the projectors of the Albany & Susquehanna line had completed it to Binghamton, they suddenly found themselves involved in all the complications and controversies of an intricate system. The intended local road was an element of strength or a source of danger not to be ignored by the managers of the great trunk lines.

Messrs. Jay Gould and James Fisk, Jr., had at this time already succeeded in firmly establishing themselves in the practical ownership of the Erie Railway. Mr. Daniel Drew, some six months before, had been driven out of its treasurership, and even Commodore Vanderbilt had been compelled by fair means and by foul to abandon all idea of controlling its management. When the Susquehanna Road was completed it became at once a most important element in the successful prosecution of the plans of Messrs. Gould and Fisk. It was so from two points of view,—either as regarded their competition with the Central Road for the carriage of the produce of the West to New England; or, still more important, as regarded their competition with other agencies for the carriage of coal to the same region. The anthracite coal deposits of America lie but a short distance to the south of the Erie Railway. Disappointed in the hope of successfully competing with the Central Road for the carriage of the produce of the West, convinced at last by hard experience that the more of this business the road undertook to do the more hopelessly bankrupt it became, the Erie managers had more and more turned their attention to the business of transporting coal. In this also they were subject to a very sharp competition, particularly from the wealthy companies which themselves owned the coal-beds, and which now proposed to supplement their business as colliers with that of carriers also. This by no means met the views of the Erie people. They were now entering into vast contracts with various coal companies to haul many hundreds of thousands of tons per annum; they naturally wished to extend their connection, as by doing so they accomplished two ends,—they shut the coal companies up in their mines, making them dependent on the Erie Railway for access to their markets, and at the same time they secured to themselves a monopoly in so far as the consumers were concerned; they, in fact, placed themselves as an indispensable medium between producer and consumer. The Albany & Susquehanna Road might well develop into an independent and competing line; hence they greatly coveted the possession of it. By it they would not only secure an access to Albany, but would forge the link which was to unite the Erie with a whole network of roads running north and east from Albany throughout coal-consuming New England.

It is wholly unnecessary to dwell upon the public considerations which rendered it unadvisable that the adventurers then representing the Erie Railway should be intrusted with a practical control over the winter supply of such an article as anthracite coal. However amiable or otherwise they might be in their domestic characters, their course had not been such as to make unprejudiced observers anxious to repose in them so delicate a duty as that of sole purveyors at any season of an article of prime necessity. The coal companies naturally did not look with any favor at a policy which threatened their lines of communication. Finally Mr. Ramsey, as the controlling influence in the Albany & Susquehanna management, neither desired to surrender the independence of his road, nor, in view of the recent experience of others, did he impose implicit faith in either the verbal or written assurances or obligations of the Erie representatives. Possession was with them considerably more than nine points of the law, and Mr. Ramsey evinced a marked repugnance to surrender the property intrusted to his charge into their possession, regardless of any liberal promises held out as to subsequent beneficial results, public and private, likely to ensue from his doing so.

The position of Mr. Ramsey in his own board of direction was not, however, perfectly secure. Certain enmities and jealousies had, little by little, not unnaturally grown up along the line of the road, and, at the election of directors in 1868, a ticket had been chosen partly in the opposition interest. What these parties represented when they came into the board it is difficult to say; it may have been a restless feeling of discontent at the slow progress of the enterprise, or a vague desire for change; or, perhaps, a personal dislike and mistrust of Mr. Ramsey. Whatever the cause, the direction at the time of the completion of the road was divided not unevenly. This condition of affairs was very unsatisfactory to Mr. Ramsey. He maintained that at the previous election he and his friends had been taken by surprise; that no wish for a change in management really existed in the minds of the bulk of the stockholders; but, finally, whether it existed or not, he let it be distinctly understood that he did not intend to belong to a divided direction, and that at the coming election either he or his opponents were to go out. The materials for a lively contest for the control of the company in September, 1869, thus existed in great abundance and on all sides.

The road was completed in January, and early in June the Erie manipulators began their preparations to obtain possession of it, or, as they more graphically would have said, to "gobble" it. The stock of the road was nominally quoted at about twenty-five per cent of its par value; it was rarely bought or sold, and was supposed to possess little real value, except as representing the control of the enterprise. It was almost exclusively in the hands of three classes of owners,—

the directors and those dwelling along the line of the road, subscribing municipalities, and certain capitalists who held it as security for money advanced and expended in construction. The subscription books of the company had never been closed, as but two million eight hundred thousand dollars of the four million dollars of authorized capital had ever been subscribed, and of the amount of stock which had been subscribed for, eight hundred thousand dollars had been forfeited in the manner already mentioned. Whoever desired to get possession of the property had, therefore, to obtain the control for a longer or shorter period, to include the election day, of a majority of this stock. The Erie party wishing to come in, and the opposition minority determined not to go out, thus had natural affinities to each other. But though when united they controlled a formidable minority of the whole stock, yet it was by no means the majority, and the Ramsey party was now thoroughly alive to the danger of the situation. The plan for the approaching campaign was soon matured. Under a sudden demand for election purposes the stock, which for years had been nominally quoted at twenty, rose rapidly in July to forty and fifty, and even to sixty and sixty-five per cent. All parties were buying. The issue was, however, to be decided by stock held by municipalities, and it was to the control of this that the greatest efforts were devoted. Here lay the stronghold of the Ramsey party; and here they felt secure, for the law authorized the town commissioners, who held this stock as trustees, to sell it only for cash and at its par value, and forbade them to sell it for less unless specially authorized to do so by a town vote. This was a point which it seemed hardly likely to touch. Suddenly, and to their great dismay, Mr. Ramsey and his friends heard of agents out among the towns offering the commissioners par for the stock, provided the offer was accepted at once. Naturally this was a great temptation to commissioners who represented towns which grievously felt the weight of railroad loans. These men were suddenly called upon to accept or reject, on their own responsibility, an offer which, a few days before, would have seemed incredible, but the acceptance of which, while it would relieve the town of debt, would also deprive it of all voice in the management of the road waited for so long. In a number of cases the commissioners considered it their duty to accept the offer, and the control of several hundred shares was in this way secured. The Ramsey party was thus forced into the field, and the stock of towns rose to a premium. This process, however, involved a very considerable outlay of money and no inconsiderable risk of loss. Buying up a majority of the stock was altogether too much like paying for a road. Why should that be obtained at great cost which could equally well be got for nothing? Stimulated by the passion which Mr. Fisk has happily described as an inherited disposition "to rescue things out of somebody else," one Sunday afternoon, early in August, a party of gentlemen met at the Fifth Avenue Hotel in New York and arranged a new plan, involving the certain transfer of the road into their hands, but avoiding the necessity of further pecuniary outlay. A negotiation was successfully concluded for the purchase of four hundred and fifty thousand dollars of the stock of various towns on the following terms: no money was to pass, but the bonds of Messrs. Gould and Fisk were given, binding them to purchase and pay for the stock after the election, provided the commissioners should at the election vote as the givers of the bond should direct. The legal effect of such an arrangement may well have escaped the town commissioners, but Messrs. Fisk and Gould had not as a rule up to this time been found deficient in matters of technical nicety. These bonds had no binding force whatever. It was not a sale for cash, it was contrary to law and to public policy; it was an arrangement wholly beyond the powers of the commissioners to make, and one which the courts would not sustain. The commissioners who accepted these bonds and who subsequently did vote as those who gave them dictated, were public officials, as such their duties were prescribed and were sufficiently simple; they could sell, and they could vote, but if they sold it was to be for cash down, and if they voted it was to be on their own judgments, and not on those of other people. In this case, indeed, what security had they that, after they had voted the road into the hands of the Erie managers, the conditions of the bond in regard to the purchase of the stock would be fulfilled? As a matter of fact they did vote as they agreed, but nothing further was ever done to complete the transfer of the stock.

Events now moved rapidly on both sides. On the 3d of August the certificates of town stock were presented for transfer. It was a new question; Mr. Ramsey was away, and the treasurer hesitated. Finally, all stock sold for cash and paid for by either side was transferred; but the transfer was denied where, in the opinion of the treasurer, the transaction was not completed. It was evident they were pressing the Ramsey party heavily. It now occurred to Ramsey that the subscription-books had never been closed, and that twelve thousand shares of the capital stock of the company were as yet unissued. On the 5th he took the subscription-book home with him, held a meeting of a few of his friends, and, among them, they wrote down their names for nine thousand five hundred shares of stock. It was fully understood that this subscription bound those who made it to no immediate payments; ten per cent was to be paid in at once, and for this Ramsey was to provide; the remainder would only be called in as should be ordered by the board of directors whom this very stock would elect. Meanwhile, if any of the subscribers desired to get rid of their stock, Ramsey undertook to relieve them of it. That this subscription, made by directors in secret on the eve of an election, and with a view of affecting that election, should have subsequently been held legal is open to criticism; its good faith even might well have been suspected; but that, on grave consideration, it should be justifiable is perhaps as severe a censure as could be passed on the condition of affairs existing in the community in which it was made. Yet, under the circumstances, unnecessary and unfortunate as the step afterwards proved to have been, Mr. Ramsey and his friends were justified in taking it. It is simply necessary to refer to those who now sought to obtain control of the Albany & Susquehanna Railroad. Their position in the community, their standing in the courts, their financial and fiduciary relations, were notorious. They had reduced society to a condition in which any man brought into conflict with them could not but realize that he had only himself to rely on, that a species of Lynch law prevailed, and that might and possession alone counted for anything. The first duty of Mr. Ramsey then, unquestionably, was to keep the property intrusted to his charge out of the hands of those men; this every consideration of honor and of responsibility bound him to do at any cost and by all legal means, certain that, whatever he might scruple at, his opponents, once in control, would scruple at nothing. This step was legal, and, however questionable in many aspects, Mr. Ramsey and his friends were justified in taking it, provided they made their subscriptions in good faith to their company, and held themselves responsible for them. At best, however, it was an error in judgment. By it Mr. Ramsey sacrificed much of the strength of his position, which lay in the fact that he was fighting men who had set the most infamous precedents ever known for transactions of a not dissimilar character. As usual in dealing in measures of questionable right and expediency, one doubtful step soon led to another which admitted of no doubt.

Ten per cent on the amount of the subscriptions had at once to be provided, and that, too, by Ramsey, whose resources were already strained to the utmost. Again he had recourse to Groesbeck, and drew on him for $100,000; he had also subscribed for more stock in Groesbeck's name. The subscription, involving as it did further possible calls to the full value of the stock, Groesbeck politely declined; the draft he honored, receiving as collateral for it a deposit of $150,000 of the equipment bonds of the Albany & Susquehanna Railroad Co., which belonged to the road, and which Mr. Ramsey procured from the treasurer for the purpose of so pledging them. The ten per cent of the subscription was thus paid in, and the nine thousand five hundred shares were placed on the books of the company to the credit of the nominal subscribers, each of whom gave Ramsey a voting proxy for the coming election. Months afterwards Mr. Groesbeck defended this transaction, and declared that, under the same circumstances and fighting the same men, he himself would have gone as far, and further too, if necessary. The proceeding was, however, none the less indefensible. The securities which had thus been misapplied were shortly after, at Groesbeck's own suggestion, returned to the officials of the company, and their place supplied by collateral of inferior value; and as for the stock, it was never voted on, and the issue of it only served to endanger the case of the Ramsey party.[1]

This took place on the 5th of August, but already the usual storm of judicial orders and injunctions had begun. The stock of the towns being, so far as possible, secured, the next blow was directed at the stock reissued and held as collateral. Two blocks of this were outstanding,—one in the hands of Chase, the other in those of Groesbeck. On the application of Messrs. Gould and Fisk's counsel, an injunction was issued by Mr. Justice Barnard, of the Supreme Court, forbidding any votes

[1] This and the previous paragraph are republished in the form in which they originally appeared. Yet it may well be questioned whether even the modified censure implied upon Mr. Ramsey's proceedings would bear examination. Ordinary rules cannot always govern exceptional cases. If a man finds himself involved in an every-day controversy, however angry, he is very properly expected to confine himself to recognized remedies; if, however, he is suddenly roused from his sleep by the assault of midnight robbers, he cannot, if he is a man of courage, be called upon to exercise any nice judgment as to the use he may make of the weapons nearest at hand;—it is a case of self-preservation. Especially would this be true if his assailants were notoriously in collusion with the watch. If Ramsey had hesitated, even for an instant, his friends would have lost courage, and he could never have recovered himself; under the circumstances it is very difficult to see why he was not as fully justified in the use of any and every weapon as a man would be in a struggle for his life. Of course in the one case or the other he would be amenable to the law for any illegal act. The question is one purely of moral accountability; legally, a man so circumstanced must act at his own peril. He may infringe laws, and, if he does, he must be prepared to undergo the penalty of so doing, but it may yet be his duty to incur that penalty in defence of his trust.

being cast upon this stock, and ordering its transfer to a receiver pending judicial investigation; all this upon the ground that the stock was unlawfully issued. The books were to close upon the 7th, the order was procured on the 4th. While this was going on in the city, the Ramsey party was not idle in the country. On the same day they appeared before Judge Parker of Owego and commenced a suit, resulting, of course, in the inevitable injunction, by which all parties were restrained and enjoined from transferring on the books of the company seven hundred shares of stock belonging to the town of Oneonta, and which the Erie party claimed to have purchased. No sooner did the news of this move arrive in New York, than Mr. Thomas G. Shearman, a member of the firm of Field, Shearman, & Co., and one of the most trusted legal advisers of those now controlling the Erie Railway, was despatched to Owego, where he succeeded in getting the injunction dissolved. Hitherto the engagement had been at long range, as it were, but it now lacked a few days only of the date when transfers previous to the election were to cease; it was time for close quarters. Not content with the success of his defensive operations, the Erie counsellor at once assumed a vigorous offensive. Two new suits were initiated,—one to compel the immediate transfer of that very Oneonta stock which the company had just previously sought to prevent; and the other, a more vital thrust still, sought to restrain Ramsey himself from the further performance of his duties as president of the company. It is almost unnecessary to say that both the desired orders were almost immediately obtained. The board of direction was divided into two hostile camps exactly equal in strength,— they stood seven to seven. The suspension of Mr. Ramsey thus turned the scale and placed the Erie opposition in the majority. It remained only to call a meeting of the directors, over which the vice-president, whose sympathy with the Erie movement was pronounced, would preside, and this meeting would vote out of office the present treasurer, who hesitated about the desired transfers, and would replace him by a suitable successor. Absolute control of the books thus secured, the election might be regarded as a mere matter of detail. All the day of that meeting the offices of the company swarmed with indignant directors and opposing counsel; angry words passed, loud threats were uttered; the suspended president was informed that his presence was undesired, and the un-suspended vice-president showed a strong disposition to assume also the duties of treasurer in so far as these involved the entering of transfers and the issuing of certificates of stock. At last a sort of tussle took place over the books, and then the police were called in, who established an angry truce. All this took place on the 5th; on the 7th the books were to be closed.

The control of those books, it was well understood, implied the control of the road. The presence of James Fisk, Jr., and of Jay Gould in the struggle was no mystery, and the officers of the road could not fail to recall how, only a few months before, the vault of the Union Pacific Railroad had been forced, in a vain search for the books of the company, under cover of a judicial process and at the dictation of these very men. That the records were not in safety while in the offices of the corporation was notorious. That night, in the presence of counsel, and with the knowledge of the treasurer, they were removed from the building. The law guaranteed to stockholders access to the books of the corporation; the judicial abuse of the processes of law had converted this right into a facility for fraud. Whether those who would now insist upon the right were likely to avail themselves of that opportunity was a question in regard to which recent experience in other quarters might warrant the formation of an opinion. In any case the books were now surreptitiously removed under the advice of counsel, and the action of the officials who assented to this removal was indorsed by public opinion, and, through-out the subsequent proceedings, was not censured by the courts.

The next day the opposition wing of the direction met and organized with the vice-president in the chair. Just as they were proceeding to business, however, an attorney of the other wing quietly entered the room and served upon four of those present a new judicial order, restraining them from acting as directors of the company, or from interfering with its affairs. This unexpected move, leaving them without a quorum, fell like a thunderbolt on the Albany members of the Erie party, and they precipitately retired from the field and took the first train to New York in search of counsel and assistance.

Reaching the Grand Opera House and the offices of the Erie counsel, the fugitives laid their case before Mr. Shearman. The quick eye of that gentleman at once took in the whole situation, and he was not unequal to the emergency. The president, vice-president, and a majority of the board of direction were now suspended, and the Albany & Susquehanna Railroad was suspended with them; every one was enjoined; there was no one authorized to give an order or to pay out a dollar; chaos was come again. Recognizing the fact that a court of equity had done this mischief through the exercise of one of its powers, Mr. Shearman was inspired with a conviction that the same court must repair it by the exercise of another power,—injunctions had occasioned the dead-lock, a receivership must dissolve it. A new suit was at once commenced, the complaint in which set forth the existing condition of affairs, and prayed for the appointment of receivers who should operate the road, and so avert the disastrous consequences otherwise sure to ensue. This paper was drawn up by Mr. Shearman at his office in the Twenty-third Street Opera House, on the afternoon of Friday the 6th of August. It was not ready for signature until the hour of ten o'clock, P.M. The Grand Opera House is not in the immediate vicinity of any court of law, nor do judges generally frequent their court-rooms at late hours on August evenings. The private residence of Mr. Justice Barnard was on Twenty-first Street, at least half a mile away, and on the morning of this day the Justice himself was at the bedside of his dying mother at Poughkeepsie, seventy-five miles from New York. Telegraphs from Mr. Fisk had, however, found him there and summoned him to the city. The order was ready for signature at 10.20 P.M., when it was delivered to a junior partner of the firm of Field,

Shearman, & Co., who thereupon left the Grand Opera House and, in fifteen minutes, returned with what purported to be Judge Barnard's signature appended to it. A strange obscurity hangs over this part of the transaction. It was never stated throughout the subsequent proceedings where this order was signed; it was never proved that it had then been signed by Judge Barnard at all. Diligent inquiry at a date long subsequent failed to discover any trace of it in the records of the court; no evidence was ever elicited that Judge Barnard was in New York at any time during that day. It was subsequently said to have been signed at the house of Fisk's mistress; but this strange statement only called forth a bare denial unaccompanied by any explanation.[2] That this order, whether there signed by him or not, was subsequently adopted as his own by Judge Barnard admits of no doubt. Under the most favorable supposition it would appear that the surprisingly brief period of fifteen minutes had sufficed to go through all the forms and make all the inquiries necessary to satisfy the judicial mind in regard to so trifling a matter as the receivership of some one hundred and fifty miles of railroad, involving millions of capital. This order appointed Charles Courter, of whom the judge probably knew absolutely nothing, and James Fisk, Jr., of whom he undoubtedly knew a great deal, receivers of the Albany & Susquehanna Railroad Co. Criticism is wholly unnecessary. The whole proceeding reflects the highest credit on the energy of all concerned: it speaks volumes. The law's delay is an ill of which the citizens of New York, certainly, have no cause to complain, at all times and under all circumstances.

By half after ten o'clock all was settled, and at eleven the

[2] It has since been stated, on the authority of Judge Barnard, that he accidentally met the counsel on his way from the cars to his house, and was asked by him to sign the order; that he did so, stepping into a neighboring real-estate office for the purpose. The meeting was certainly a singular coincidence, and the method indicated of transacting judicial business of the first importance is calculated to excite surprise, if not consternation. The "explanation" seems, however, to have been considered perfectly satisfactory by those to whom it was made.

two receivers, accompanied by a select body-guard of directors, friends, and lawyers, were on their way by the night train to take possession of their charge. Their opponents had, however, already got an inkling of the summary process impending over them from New York, and, while Mr. Shearman was busy with the preparation of his order in the Grand Opera House, other counsel were no less busy in the opposing camp at Albany preparing a counter-order, appointing another receiver in their own interest. This, when completed, was duly submitted to Mr. Justice Peckham, of the Supreme Court of the Albany district, between nine and ten o'clock of the same (Friday) evening. The signature of this magistrate was affixed to it, and a Mr. Pruyn, of Albany, was by him appointed receiver of the Albany & Susquehanna Railroad Co. It was close work. Each order took effect when signed, and there certainly was no delay in their preparation, and even less in procuring signatures to them. The evidence seemed subsequently to indicate that the Albany receivership had about one hour's priority in time; it had, however, one hundred and fifty miles of distance in its favor, and the great weight which attaches to possession as an element of success in litigation has long since passed into a proverb.

Thus, on Saturday, the 7th of August, everything indicated a collision of forces. No sooner had Receiver Fisk reached Albany, and received the reports of his scouts, than he hastened with his friends to the offices of the company. He arrived there towards eight o'clock. In spite of this praiseworthy activity on their part, Messrs. Fisk and Courter, on proceeding to take possession of the premises, encountered a somewhat unexpected obstacle in the person of a Mr. Van Valkenburg, the superintendent of the road, who, upon being informed of their errand. announced that he was already in possession under the orders of Receiver Pruyn, and further intimated that he did not propose to abandon it. A very amusing and somewhat exciting scene then ensued. The junior appointee of Mr. Justice Barnard presented his papers to the superintendent, seated himself on the table, announced himself as Mr. James Fisk, Jr., of New York, come to take possession and prepared to do so if it required "millions of money and an unlimited number of men." He further added that this was his twenty-sixth raid of the same character, and that he proposed "to take you fellows"; to all of which Mr. Van Valkenburg pleasantly replied that he "hoped he would have a good time doing it." His companions Mr. Fisk introduced as his "boys," and invited them in to possess themselves. Quite a lively colloquy ensued, which was not satisfactory to Mr. Fisk, who from words gradually proceeded to overt acts, and finally ordered his "boys" to put the other "boys" out. Unfortunately the preponderance of force was not on his side. Instead of ejecting his opponents, he was summarily ejected himself, and, after being ignominiously and very roughly hustled down stairs, he found himself in the street in a very dishevelled condition. Nor did his discomfiture stop here; no sooner did he reach the pavement than he was arrested by a fiery little individual, claiming to be a policeman, and ignominiously marched off to the station-house. As no complaint was preferred he was speedily released, but probably not until he had discovered that his arrest, like his ejectment, was the work, not of a policeman, but of an employee of the company. No sooner was he again a free man than he returned to the charge. Mr. Pruyn was now at the offices in person, claiming to be in possession as receiver, and a crowd of lawyers, officers, and parties in interest had also assembled there. The heads of the opposing factions met face to face. No further riotous demonstrations were attempted, but, pending advices from New York, Mr. Fisk kept up the semblance of a possession. He evidently bore no ill-will to Mr. Van Valkenburg, on account of the rough treatment of the morning, as he even went so far as to compliment that gentleman on his display of energy, and to signify a desire to extend to him his personal favor. As to Mr. Ramsey, Mr. Fisk, as a happy solution of existing complications, suggested that the possession of the road should be decided, not as of old by a personal contest between the two heads of the opposing factions, but by the goddess of chance, or whatever other divinity may preside over the issue of a game of "seven up"; and, with such interchange of amenities and pleasant sallies of wit, with now and again the service of some notice or order of court, and perhaps an injunction or two, the *protégé* of Barnard beguiled the weary monotony of the day.

The cessation of active hostilities did not last long. The discomfiture of the morning had been at once telegraphed to Mr. Shearman, in the recesses of the Grand Opera House, and that gentleman had forthwith proceeded to discover and apply the suitable remedies of the law. Recourse was at once had, or is alleged to have been had, to Judge Barnard, sitting at special term in the court-house. Again, however, a curious obscurity hangs over the actual whereabouts of that magistrate. On this day his mother was still lingering at Poughkeepsie, and another judge was sitting at special term in the court-house. In any case a most unusual and indeed wellnigh antiquated writ, never before granted to meet such an exigency as that which had now arisen, was at once exhumed and prepared. In the first place a new and sweeping injunction, purporting to have been granted by Judge Barnard, was obtained, by virtue of which Mr. Receiver Pruyn, the sheriff of the county, the Albany police, and all the railroad employees, were restrained from any interference with receivers Courter and Fisk. Not satisfied with this, a writ of assistance [3] was likewise ordered to issue, by which the sheriff, and, if need be, the *posse comitatus,* were placed at the disposal of Messrs. Fisk and Courter. This was a sufficiently unusual proceeding, but the service of the process was so extraordinary that the ordering it was at once reduced to the commonplace. Now, probably for the

[3] "Writs to the sheriff, to assist a receiver, sequestrator, or other party to a suit in chancery, to get possession, under a decree of the court, of lands withheld from him by another party to the suit. These writs, which issue from the equity side of the Court of Exchequer, or from any other court of chancery, are at least as old as the reign of James I., and are still in common use in England, Ireland, and some of the United States."— *Quincy's (Mass.) Reports,* p. 396.

first time on record, both injunction and writ were forwarded to their destination for service by electric telegraph. That afternoon officers in Albany actually undertook to serve upon parties to a suit processes which had been issued in New York not an hour before, on the strength of affidavits as to facts which had that day occurred in Albany. In place of making service with the original, bearing the seal of the court and the signature of the judge, the very ink of the copies which the officers had in their hands was not yet dry. Of course such a service was contemptuously disregarded, nor did the sheriff presume to insist upon it.

It was now afternoon, and it was very evident that nothing further could be effected this day; both parties, however, claimed to be in possession, and neither would yield the ground. Finally a species of truce was arranged to hold good over the coming Sunday. A representative of each party was to be left in the offices, and, before nine o'clock of the coming Monday, no act of hostility, open or covert, in so far as possession was concerned, was to be attempted by either side.

The interval of Sunday was passed in active preparation. While the representatives of the receivers tarried in the deserted offices, the principals themselves were busy with their plans of campaign. Mr. Fisk and his friends among the directors retired to New York to get advice and the originals of the telegraphed writs; Mr. Pruyn and the Ramsey party stoutly prepared themselves in Albany for such trials as the morrow might bring forth. The issue now presented was, in plain language, one simply of judicial nerve. It was a conflict between the judiciary of New York City and that of the country. The system of electing judges by the popular vote had at last brought forth bitter fruit, and men had been elevated to the bench who should have ornamented the dock. These selections did not perhaps extend beyond one or two districts out of the eight into which the State was divided, but each of the thirty-three judges who composed those eight courts exercised throughout the State the extensive and delicate powers of a chancellor. All were magistrates of co-ordinate powers, and technically of one court; an order made by one could be dissolved by another, an officer appointed by this magistrate could be suspended in the exercise of his duties by that, what one justice could do the next could undo. Everything under such a system depended on judicial respect for judicial action; courtesy and confidence were the essence of it. All these had, in certain quarters, now long passed away. The judges of the country had felt bitterly the discredit brought upon the common bench by the action of more than one judge in the city; there were among them those who had been deeply mortified by a contemptuous disregard of their process. Hence a conflict had become inevitable, and nowhere was it so likely to arise as out of the litigations originating with the managers of the Erie Railway. A peculiar discredit had now long attached to these, and certain names, both on the bench and at the bar, were always associated with them. There are facts which are of public notoriety; the community recognizes them and no justice can ignore them. When, therefore, James Fisk, Jr., was appointed, as a matter of course, by Judge Barnard, receiver of a railway, no part of which lay within a hundred miles of that magistrate's judicial district, and when this appointment was made on the eve of a contested election for directors of that railway, and must have been decisive of the contest, then, at last, a case was presented which could not be ignored. The conflict was not likely to be a pleasant one. Recent proceedings in other causes had indicated with sufficient clearness the lengths to which certain justices of the first district were not indisposed to go. Neither the scandal certainly involved, nor the defeat not unlikely to ensue, were pleasant to contemplate; but the stand must be made. Circumstances had already designated Judge Peckham, of Albany, as the magistrate to whom the Ramsey people must almost necessarily have recourse. The public estimation in which this gentleman is held was shown by his election, shortly after the events here narrated took place, as one of the new Court of Appeals organized under the judiciary clause of the rejected Constitution of 1869. The scandal which arose out of the Albany & Susquehanna case most materially contributed to the adoption of this single clause. It is probable, therefore, that the action of Judge Peckham on this occasion had a direct influence on his own future elevation; it certainly received the public indorsement.

Receiver Fisk might confidently be expected back, well armed with injunctions and with the original of his writ of assistance on Monday morning. It was necessary that Receiver Pruyn should be prepared to meet him. The last New York suit had enjoined the Albany receiver from any interference with the New York receivers, and had been accompanied by a writ of assistance. This was now met in the usual way. A new Albany suit enjoined the New York receiver from any interference with Mr. Pruyn, and at the same time an order was issued by Judge Peckham restraining the sheriffs from taking any action under the writs of assistance. It was further sought to punish Mr. Fisk for a contempt of court in interfering with its receiver on the previous Saturday, but this the judge held it necessary to send to a referee to take evidence and report. A temporary injunction was granted, and Mr. Fisk was ordered to appear and show cause on the 13th why this should not be made permanent. Such were the legal complications encountered by Mr. Fisk on his return to the scene of his labors early on Monday morning. He had left New York on the boat the evening before, in company with fifteen friends and advisers, and was fully prepared for vigorous operations. The condition of affairs did not look propitious. He was distinctly checkmated at Albany, and the order checkmating him, and forbidding the sheriffs to interfere to put him in possession, was already on the express-train which had left Albany at 8 A.M., and would be due in Binghamton, at the other end of the coveted road, at three o'clock that afternoon. A party to a conflict, however, who operates by steam, is at a manifest disadvantage when acting against one who despatches writs by telegraph. In the present case Mr. Fisk, baffled at one end of the line, went vigorously to work a hundred and forty miles away at the other end of it. While the express-train was toiling along to Binghamton, enjoining as it went all sheriffs and others from paying any attention to his writs of assistance, the telegraph was flashing those writs direct to Binghamton, and commanding that immediate possession should be given to his representatives. Accordingly just before two o'clock, and as the afternoon train for Albany was on the point of leaving Binghamton, the sheriff of Broome County made his appearance, and, by virtue of a writ of Judge Barnard's, fresh from the telegraph wires, proceeded to take possession of all the property of the Albany & Susquehanna Railroad Co., including the train then standing at the station. Three locomotives belonging to the same company were also at Binghamton. These he undertook to seize next; of two of them he obtained possession, but the agent of the road was before him with the third; for, just as he was approaching his prey, writ in hand and borne upon one locomotive, the ingenious employee switched him off, and, while his own path suddenly led into space, he saw his prize gently slide down the grade out of his reach, and there get up the steam necessary to make good its escape.

The Barnard receivers were thus fairly installed in possession of the Binghamton end of the road, of the point where it connected with the Erie. An assistant superintendent of the Erie Railway was at once appointed superintendent of the Albany & Susquehanna, and a conductor of the same road was ordered to take out the regular train to Albany, which was still standing at the platform where it was seized. Matters were evidently approaching a crisis. Different sets of receivers were operating the two ends of the road, and two sheriffs, bearing conflicting processes, were rapidly approaching each other on trains drawn by the locomotives and directed by the officers of the hostile factions. This condition of affairs was telegraphed to the Ramsey train at Harpersville, twenty-five miles from Binghamton, and, after some consideration, it was determined to proceed no farther. Meanwhile the news of the Binghamton proceedings caused Superintendent Van Valkenburg to decide on vigorous measures. In the first place he proceeded to clear the offices of all hostile influences. Mr. Fisk had not that day been allowed within the premises. Repeatedly, in company with the sheriff and others, had he presented himself and energetically demanded admission. It was of no avail. It was different with Mr. Courter, his fellow-receiver; he had been treated with a degree of courtesy, and indeed had been permitted to sustain the character of a nominal receiver within the offices. This gentleman was, however, now notified by Mr. Van Valkenburg that the farce of a double possession was to terminate then and there. On Saturday, in the little unpleasantness with Mr. Fisk, Van Valkenburg had given some indications that he was a man of few words and decided action. The hint had not been thrown away. Mr. Courter, after a formal resistance just sufficient to establish the fact of forcible ejectment, withdrew from the premises, and the Barnard receivers abandoned every pretence of actual possession of the Albany end of the line. Van Valkenburg's next move was to telegraph an order over the road, stopping every train where it then was; all movement was thus brought to a stand. An extra train, carrying a hundred and fifty men from the workshops, under command of the master mechanic, was then sent up the road to be ready for any emergency. Having thus cleared everything away for action, the next move of the other side was in order.

The representatives of this other side were meanwhile advancing from the opposite direction; upon the train were the sheriff of Broome County, the Erie superintendent of the road, and some twenty men. As they moved along, the orders of Judge Barnard were served at each way station, the old officials of the road were displaced, and Erie men were substituted for them. So eager, indeed, was the sheriff in the discharge of his duties, under the electro-writ of assistance, that he not only served an order, the illegal character of which he must have more than suspected, throughout his own county, but he continued to do so throughout the adjacent county, and, indeed, seemed not indisposed to extend his bailiwick to

Albany. At Afton, about thirty miles from Binghamton, a despatch was received from Mr. Van Valkenburg, notifying the party that any farther advance would be at its own peril. The Albany people were then lying at Bainbridge, six miles farther down the track. After some hesitation, which involved a great deal of rapid telegraphing and no inconsiderable delay, positive orders for an advance came to the Erie party, followed shortly after by reinforcements. It was now deep in the night, but the train at last was started, and moved slowly and cautiously towards Bainbridge. The Albany party was prepared to receive it. They lay on a siding, with a patent frog —a little machine made to slide trains on to the rails, but equally calculated to slide them off—attached at a convenient point to the main track. In total ignorance of this bit of strategy, the Erie people felt their way along, when, just as Bainbridge, to their very great relief, seemed safely reached, their locomotive gently and suddenly glided off the track, and their train was brought to a stand-still. The instant this took place the Albany train moved up the siding, passed triumphantly by its disabled opponents and on to the main track above them, where it took its position in their rear, effectually cutting off all retreat. As the Erie party tumbled out of their train, they were met by Mr. Smith, one of the counsel of their opponents, who glanced at the process under which they were acting, and at once pronounced it worthless. There was no alternative; they had fallen into a trap, unconditional surrender was all that remained. This was accordingly submitted to, and Sheriff Browne of Broome County, and all his *posse comitatus,* were helped off their train and duly served with the order of Judge Peckham, restraining them from doing or attempting anything in aid of the receivers appointed by Judge Barnard.

Having disposed of this little party by capture, and it being now broad day, the Ramsey commander decided vigorously to follow up his advantage, steaming up the road towards Binghamton. On the way he displaced the recently appointed Fisk men, and replaced the ejected Ramsey men in charge of the various stations. Everything proceeded well until the train approached the long tunnel, near Binghamton. This was the battle-ground chosen by the Erie party. Here, close to their base of operations, and near their supplies, they had massed their reserves, after the total and ignominious capture of their advance guard.

The tunnel is some twenty-two hundred feet in length, and is about fifteen miles from Binghamton. It marks the last summit the road crosses in going west, and, on either side, is approached by a heavy ascending grade and round a sharp curve. The Albany party arrived at this point at about ten o'clock, and here halted. On the other side of the hill, trains were bringing up workmen from the Erie shops, under the officers of the Erie road, until Mr. Fisk's threat in regard to "any number of men" seemed tolerably certain to be verified. It was a motley collection, the control of which must have considerably puzzled the general superintendent of the Erie Railway, who found himself in command. A more unwieldy body could not well have been got together. The men were wholly unarmed, except, perhaps, with sticks, which one party was detailed to cut in the neighboring woods; they had been hastily summoned from the shops, and were ignorant as children of the crazy errand they were about, nor had they the slightest enmity towards those opposite to whom they stood in ludicrous array. This, however, was not the case with the Susquehanna people. They were now thoroughly stirred up and ready for anything. Most of them had for years been in the employ of the road, and many were personally attached to Mr. Ramsey; they regarded the effort to dispossess him as aimed also at themselves. They were, too, flushed with the success at Bainbridge, and possessed with a strong *esprit de corps*. Such being the opposing elements, they lay waiting for peremptory orders, which in any case had to come from Albany, for there both Fisk and Van Valkenburg kept their head-quarters. From time to time reinforcements came up, until by seven o'clock the Erie party was raised to an unwieldy mob of some eight hundred men, while their opponents numbered hardly less than four hundred and fifty. The Erie people now decided to try an advance, and accordingly a train well loaded with combatants was set in motion. It moved slowly through the tunnel and emerged safely from the eastern end, merely having to replace a single rail. This done, the advance was continued. Meanwhile the Albany people were fully notified of the impending danger. Accordingly, when the Erie people had replaced the rail and started, they started too, and thus the first intimation the raiders had of danger was the discovery, on rounding the sharp curve, of an approaching locomotive, angrily puffing up the grade, and apparently bent on mischief. This was more than they were prepared for. Their whistle at once signalled danger, which the Albany locomotive replied to by signalling to them to get out of the way. In vain the Erie conductor jumped off his train and gesticulated like a madman; in vain the Erie engineer tried to back out of the way; the curve was here so sharp and the incline up which it was necessary to back in order to return into the tunnel was so great, that it was instantly evident, not only that the Albany people wanted a collision, but that their wish was to be gratified. Though the Erie engine could not reverse, it had stopped, and the heavy grade kept down the speed of the Albany train, so that the collision rather indicated an *animus* than inflicted an injury; nevertheless, in a moment the two locomotives came together with a sharp shock. The damage done was not great; guards and cow-catchers were swept away, head-lights were broken, and the attacking locomotive was roughly thrown from the track; but the collision of engines was the signal for a collision of men. Before the trains had met they were emptied of their loads. Such a system of opposition was something on which the Erie people had not counted, and when, simultaneously with the collision, the Albany men rushed upon them with loud shouts, they were at once completely demoralized, and broke into a precipitate flight. Their locomotive, with broken lights and a pistol-bullet through its cab, vigorously reversed, until it had reversed itself out of the *mêlée* and back into the tunnel, while they themselves took to their heels and scampered back towards Binghamton. A few remained on board the train, a few stumbled back through the darkness of the tunnel, but the greater part, to whom their terror perhaps lent wings, scaled the mountain like a sand-hill in their flight.

Victory had again rested on the Albany banners; the Ramsey star was in the decided ascendant. While one party of the Albany men followed up the disorganized enemy, others busied themselves in getting the locomotive on the track. This was soon done, and then they, in their turn, locomotive and all, advanced through the tunnel to complete the rout of Erie. The last-named party had, however, rallied a little in the breathing-time afforded them, and were now at least equal to the task of making a very considerable noise. This, it is true, was not much, but in the growing darkness it was enough. In fact it might be said that one party was afraid to go forward, and the other did not dare to attack. The element of the ludicrous was becoming very pronounced, notwithstanding the earnestness of the combatants. Thus, as the shades of night deepened, they stood apart and defied each other with loud shouts and excessive profanity. A few conflicts of the more daring, a few scattering pistol-shots, a few wounds, none of them serious, told the whole story. Yet it was a riot, and a shockingly lawless one; nay, more, it was an alarming one. It was not a sudden fight between ignorant and angry mobs; it was the attempt of two great corporations to levy war on each other with organized force. How far it might have gone cannot be said, for, in the midst of the tumult, the drums of the Forty-fourth Regiment of State Militia were heard approaching, and at this not unwelcome sound the combatants desisted. The Erie people held possession of the field. The Albany party sullenly withdrew, locomotive and all, through the tunnel, which they blocked up with a freight-car, and then, after breaking down a trestle-work or two, with a view of preventing another attack, they retired to Harpersville, where they established themselves for the night.

Meanwhile the whole State was in an uproar over the scandal of these lawless acts. All along the line of the road, and indeed almost everywhere, the feeling was strongly in sympathy with Mr. Ramsey. It could not well be otherwise; without knowing anything of the circumstances of the particular case, a strong presumption was now inevitable wherever the Erie management made its appearance in any complication. At Albany the public sentiment was peculiarly strong; meetings were held, a perfect ovation greeted the arrival of the runaway locomotive from Binghamton and the captured Erie train; crowds collected round the station, and were addressed from the cars by city demagogues on their way "to the front." At last, also, the point was reached at which, if the authorities did not interfere, the people would organize and take matters into their own hands. The militia had already been called upon by the civil authorities of Broome County and had responded to the call, and now Governor Hoffman was recalled from his summer sojourning-place by telegraph, and reached Albany at almost the very time that the Forty-fourth Regiment arrived at the scene of riot. He at once took decisive measures. Orders were telegraphed to the sheriffs along the line of the road, directing them, in all cases of doubt, to treat any party in actual possession under a judicial order as being in rightful possession. The military were to be called upon only in case of extreme emergency, but, if the disorders continued, the whole district was to be placed under martial law.

In spite of these new developments, the Erie party was neither discouraged nor idle. The papers of Tuesday contained a long letter from Mr. James Fisk, Jr., setting forth at great length the magnitude of the public interests for which he claimed to be contending. The literary shortcomings of this production were excused on the ground of "quick, sharp work on a stamping ground new to me." Not content with this bid for moral support, on the evening of Tuesday, when the offices of the company would naturally have been deserted, Fisk and Courter made another effort to obtain possession of them. Armed with an order of Judge Barnard's, staying all proceedings under Judge Peckham's writ of Monday, and further fortified with an additional writ of assistance, the brother receivers made their appearance in a carriage accompanied by the sheriff. Van Valkenburg was, however, on the ground, and, for a moment or two, things had an unpleasant look; so unpleasant, indeed, that Mr. Fisk now changed his tactics. Instead of bullying he attempted bribing; all the braggart confidence of Saturday was gone, and his demeanor was chiefly marked by an excessive care for his personal safety. As for the sheriff, the indications of violence were sufficiently pronounced to induce him to think it inexpedient to proceed further. Probably they would have gone away empty-handed, had not a new judicial power just then stepped into the arena. This was Mr. Justice Clute, of the Albany County Court, who issued his order directing the arrest of the Barnard receivers for conspiring to take possession of the Albany & Susquehanna Railroad by force of arms. In obedience to this order the two indignant receivers were at once taken to Judge Clute's office, whence they were not released until they gave bail for their appearance next morning. The *coup de main* was a failure; but Mr. Fisk relieved his feelings by graphically describing the attempts which had been made to assassinate him.

The next morning Judge Peckham began the day, not exactly by setting aside his brother Barnard's recent orders, but, more courteously, by fixing a day on which cause should be shown why they should not be vacated, and, meanwhile, granting a temporary stay of all proceedings under them. The judicial equilibrium was thus restored. At last Governor Hoffman put a final stop to the judicial farce by notifying the sheriff of Albany that he was included in the directions of the previous day. The Ramsey party, being in actual possession at Albany under a judicial order, forthwith applied to the police for protection, which was immediately granted them. Meanwhile, Governor Hoffman received information of the tunnel conflict. He at once notified the counsel that such proceedings must stop, and that some agreement must be arrived at. In due time the counsel notified the Governor, in reply, that they were utterly unable to agree on anything.

His Excellency thereupon very emphatically and very properly replied that he neither knew nor cared anything for their complications, but he did propose to preserve the public peace. If those interested could not agree on some other course, it only remained for him to declare the whole district in a state of insurrection, and to operate the road as a military one. This declaration produced a document, signed by all the receivers, requesting his Excellency, as a species of nondescript superintendent, mutally agreed upon, to take possession of and operate the road. This very anomalous trust was accepted by Governor Hoffman, who issued a *quasi* military order, detailing Inspector-General McQuade as his deputy superintendent, and directing him to take possession. This was certainly a fitting climax to all that had gone before. A receiver is an officer of the court. His possession is the possession of the court. The courts in this case were fighting over the control of a railroad, and were forced to ask the Executive to hold the bone of contention while the judiciary "had it out" amongst themselves. Thus the Executive, in the utter break-down of the law, had to accept a trust which did not belong to it, and proceed to perform duties which it had no right to perform, under an authority conferred by certain persons who had no such authority to confer. And all this because a man was selected in caucus and elected at the polls a judge in the first judicial district of New York, who fairly represented the moral and intellectual level of the majority of the voters who had elevated him into infamy. It was no accident; there was no element of chance in the case; it was the working of a system which produced a logical and natural result.

Though the possession of the road was thus disposed of, certain little outstanding accounts remained to be adjusted. The vacating of Judge Peckham's orders by Judge Barnard, and the staying of proceedings under Judge Barnard's orders by Judge Peckham, were matters of too common occurrence to call for notice. The interference of Judge Clute, however, a mere county judge, was something "most tolerable and not to be endured." And now for the first time in these proceedings Judge Barnard appeared upon the stage as something more than a name. The funeral of his mother had taken place at Poughkeepsie on the previous day; on that day, also, orders had been forthcoming from him in these Susquehanna suits, purporting to be granted on the behest of Mr. Shearman, between 11 A.M. and 1 P.M., at special term at the court-house in New York City. The minutes of the court-house show that the special term at the court-house in New York City was held on this day by another magistrate. Upon the morning of the 11th, however, he at length appeared in proper person, and, after obtaining from him the usual order, setting aside Judge Peckham's action of the day before, Mr. David Dudley Field, of counsel for the Erie Railway, read to the court the return of the sheriff, setting forth the resistance he had encountered on the previous afternoon in his attempt on the Susquehanna offices. Upon his motion the court ordered a peremptory writ, not bailable, to issue, commanding the sheriff to arrest Messrs. Pruyn, Ramsey, and Van Valkenburg, and to produce their bodies in court without delay. Under this process these gentlemen were arrested that afternoon, while in the Executive Chamber, and were held in duress awaiting conveyance to New York. Of course they none of them, at this time, seriously contemplated any such journey. Recourse was again had to Judge Clute, and the non-bailable prisoners were carried before that magistrate on a *habeas corpus*. The subject was taken under consideration by him until next morning. The opponents of Mr. Fisk had shown themselves not inapt scholars, and it naturally occurred to them that processes for contempt might be made to apply to him as well as to themselves. The same thought suggested itself to Mr. Fisk, as soon as he found time to relax from the efforts incident to "quick, sharp work on a stamping ground new to him." He had once before fled to Jersey City, pursued by Barnard; he now incontinently retired to New York, terrified by Peckham. In fact, he abandoned his new "stamping ground" with great precipitation. Flying on board his own steamer, which was lying in the stream ready to serve either as an ark of refuge or a stronghold for prisoners, he was conveyed at once to New York, where he secured himself in the recesses of Castle Erie.

The next morning Judge Clute incontinently discharged the prisoners held under Judge Barnard's writ. It is almost unnecessary to say that his action was apparently in disregard of law; these proceedings throughout were open to this criticism. It was perfectly proper for Judge Clute to issue his writ of *habeas corpus;* when it came, however, to releasing prisoners held by a sheriff on a writ issued for contempt from a court superior to his own, the action of his Honor was, perhaps, more spirited than correct in practice. The prisoners, however, were released, and it only remained for the sheriff to make a return of the facts by mail to Judge Barnard. The matter was then brought once more before that magistrate, this time by Mr. Shearman. The colloquy that then took place was characteristic and well calculated to fill with terror the hearts of Peckham and Clute, no less than of Pruyn and Ramsey. The counsel began with a comparison. Judge Peckham, it appeared, had signed certain of his orders at his office; Judge Barnard, it will be remembered, was supposed to have signed his somewhere in the immediate neighborhood of a theatre. Bearing these facts in mind, one cannot but appreciate the delicate sense of honor implied in the following opening remark of the counsel: "Unlike our opponents, who invite the judge to their private office, and from which he issues his orders as if from the court, we have never sought to consult your Honor in private, and whatever we have asked has been asked openly in court, and in accordance with our firm conviction of our legal rights." The peculiarly elevated tone of Judge Barnard's court being thus established, the colloquy proceeded as follows:—

Judge Barnard. I have been looking into this matter with some degree of care, and am of opinion that J. H. Clute, signing himself as county judge of Albany County, entertained jurisdiction of this matter as a criminal contempt, well knowing that it was a civil contempt. I am not quite sure but he should be brought before me to be punished for contempt.

Mr. Shearman. I intend to follow these men as I have followed others. Four months ago we were in pursuit of certain parties, and they were finally overtaken as their coat-tails were disappearing behind a safe. I shall follow these men, if it is necessary and possible, to the end of time.

Judge Barnard. I have some years to sit on this bench, and would as soon devote them to this as to anything else.

Mr. Shearman. I am a young man also, having perhaps forty years at my disposal, and I am willing to devote them all to the pursuit of these men.

The first step in this forty years of persistent strife was thereupon at once taken by directing the sheriff to make a more detailed return. The individuals in question had, however, already fled the State, and Judge Barnard does not seem finally to have made up his mind to try conclusions with Judge Clute. Meanwhile the friends of the fugitives began to think that these proceedings had exceeded the limits of a jest. To fly the State was an ignominious thing; it seemed to imply a confession of wrong-doing; it could only be justified by the uncertainty which existed in regard to the limits of judicial power in cases of contempt, and especially of the exercise of that power by Barnard himself. He had indicated his *animus* by his remarks in court. Resort was had to negotiation. One of the Ramsey counsel went to New York and threw himself in Barnard's way. The Judge assured him that there was no vindictiveness in his mind, and this interview led finally to some distinct understanding, reassured by which the fugitives one by one came back and presented themselves in court. After this the matter took the usual course. A reference was ordered, a mass of evidence was taken, the case dragged its slow length along, bail was reduced, a multiplicity of orders were issued, the wrath of Barnard gradually subsided, and, at last, the battle of the judges died away in a faint rumble of evidence, affidavits, explanations, and orders, and then was heard of no more.

One further order, and one only, was made at about this time, to which subsequent events lent a deep consequence. The Erie party had been completely foiled in its efforts to get possession of the much-coveted books. Now and again they would obtain some clew which led them to suspect their presence somewhere, but when they were sought they were gone. Agents went out of the State hunting for them, parties were examined in the State concerning them; a strange ignorance apparently existed as to their whereabouts. They seemed ubiquitous; at one time in Albany, at another in Pittsfield, and then suddenly in Troy; but always in the undisturbed possession of some friend of Mr. Ramsey. The Erie party was, in their absence, wholly unable to estimate its own relative strength as compared with that of its opponents. It was known, however, that a portion of the forfeited stock had been reissued, and now stood in the names of Leonard, Groesbeck, and others. Leonard was a director, and in negotiating the sale for the company of certain of its second mortgage bonds and stock had reserved to himself a portion of the stock as a species of brokerage commission. Mr. Leonard, however, was one of the directors in close sympathy and alliance with the Erie management, and, in regard to the stock reissued and standing in his name, for which in reality no consideration had been paid to the company, it seemed unnecessary to institute any proceedings. Not so as regarded that issued to Groesbeck and paid for by him. The reissue of this last stock was pronounced flagrantly illegal and void, and Judge Barnard was accordingly petitioned to appoint a receiver for it. The order was immediately granted, and Mr. William J. A. Fuller, an individual who had once been a clerk in Mr. Field's office, was named receiver, and directed to take immediate possession of the property. Armed with this order, and accompanied by a sheriff's officer, the new receiver proceeded at once to Mr. Groesbeck's office and demanded his scrip. Upon Mr. Groesbeck's demurring somewhat at being deprived of his property in this summary way, Receiver Fuller proceeded to explain to him the mysterious terrors of a writ of assistance, which

almost unknown process he darkly intimated he had somewhere at hand. Mr. Groesbeck was tolerably familiar from
long experience with all the usual judicial processes which are
auxiliary to New York financial combinations, but writs of assistance were implements strange to him. The element of the
unknown seems to have produced the desired effect, and Mr.
Groesbeck delivered to Mr. Fuller certificates for nine hundred
shares of stock. Under the same authority this gentleman
further collected other certificates representing sixteen hundred additional shares. His duty was simply, at the most, to
hold these shares pending the result of litigation as to the
legality of their issue; he subsequently, as will be seen, took
what may be called very enlarged views of these duties. Both
parties had now gathered up their strength for the election
which was to take place on the 7th of September.

It was provided in the by-laws of the company that the polls
should be opened at twelve o'clock on the day of election, and
should continue open for one hour; no transfers of shares were
to take place during the thirty days next preceding the election; three inspectors were provided for, to be chosen each
year by the stockholders; it was their duty to conduct the
election; they were to be provided by the secretary with a
list of stockholders entitled to vote, and to them also upon
that day the transfer book was to be submitted. To this state
of the law and the facts the two parties prepared to conform
their plans. It was in the first place incumbent on the Ramsey party to restore the books to the offices of the company.
This was done very secretly on the night preceding the election. A certain fictitious consequence was sought to be attached to the way in which this was done, owing to the fact
that, when the messengers arrived with the books, instead
of finding everything quiet and deserted as they had hoped,
they discovered a large crowd gathered in front of the offices
watching a conflagration across the river. The nature of their
business was thus sure to be discovered. This was just what
they wished to avoid. After a moment's reflection it was decided to drive with the books to the rear of the building and

put them in through a window. A basket and cord were found, the books were hauled up to the second-story window by the secretary, and by him secured in the safe of the company. Had the books, under the circumstances, been carried in through the front door, an officer armed with a warrant, and accompanied, if need be, by pick-locks and blacksmiths, would, in all probability, have been after them before morning. As it was, their return was a secret until it ceased to be of importance. Many unjustifiable features were assigned to the proceeding by the Fisk counsel; the one thoroughly unjustifiable one in their eyes was probably its success. It was never denied that the secretary of the company had, after the removal of the books and while they were secreted, made many entries in them. These, however, were all of transactions concluded prior to the day when the books were to be closed, and included all of those transactions, whether favoring Ramsey or Fisk. Though much was hinted in regard to these entries, during the searching investigation they were subjected to in the subsequent trial, no instance of abuse of trust was even specifically alleged, much less proved. Nor indeed is it probable in itself that any such improper entries were made, as those who made them must at the time have known that they were unnecessary so far as securing a majority of the stock was concerned.

The aspect of affairs was not, on the whole, propitious to the Erie party as the day of election drew near. Their opponents held the books, which forced them to act very much in the dark, and the inspectors of election were understood to incline to the Ramsey interest. That a majority of the stock also inclined to it was a matter of less moment. The situation was full of difficulty; but the men called upon to meet it were full of resource. Their preliminary step was naturally to lay in a sufficient supply of judicial orders. The regular inspectors must, in the first place, be got out of the way. It was ascertained that they were not stockholders; the by-laws required that the inspectors should be chosen from among the stockholders. The Fisk-Gould counsel at once applied to

Judge Clerke, a colleague of Judge Barnard's, in the First District, and that magistrate granted, as a matter of course, an *ex parte* order, restraining the inspectors from acting as such. Having obtained this process from Judge Clerke, and filed it away for use at the proper moment, the counsel next applied to Judge Barnard. They quietly commenced a suit in the name of the Albany & Susquehanna Railroad Co. against Messrs. Ramsey, Pruyn, Phelps, and Smith, the president, receiver, secretary, and leading counsel of the company, to recover damages for the abstraction of its books. On this complaint they obtained from Judge Barnard, on the evening of the day preceding the election, an order of arrest against the defendants, with bail fixed at $25,000. This, be it remembered, was a judicial proceeding in New York, and not in Constantinople. Thus panoplied in orders, all parties repaired on the 6th to Albany. Mr. David Dudley Field came from the pleasant shades of his summer retreat among the hills of Berkshire, and Mr. Shearman, his associate in the practice of the law, had, for the nonce, quitted his offices in the Grand Opera House, in order himself to be at the right hand of his chief in conducting those delicate proceedings so skilfully and secretly planned in New York. The former gentleman was doubtless actuated only by a high sense of his professional duty to his clients, but Mr. Shearman may have been braced for the approaching crisis by the fell purpose he had recently avowed of pursuing even for forty years the miscreants who had failed properly to respect the orders of the distinguished magistrate with whom his own relations were such models of propriety. Having arrived in Albany, the last-named gentleman repaired at once to the capitol, where he carefully informed himself as to the details of the election. This done, a general conference was held at the Delavan House, and the plan of operations was matured. The first object was to secure the organization of the meeting; that once done, arrangements of a satisfactory nature had been made to hold it. The trap was to be sprung just before the hour appointed for the election, when the regular inspectors were to be enjoined by the service upon them of Judge Clerke's *ex parte* order. The whole regular machinery being thus dislocated, a preliminary organization was to be effected, three new and thoroughly sound inspectors were to be chosen, which would insure the control of the election and the subsequent possession of the Susquehanna Railway. Every detail was arranged, every person who was to play a part was designated and carefully taught his *rôle*. Such was the extreme caution used that Mr. Shearman himself wrote out the appropriate resolutions, and indorsed upon them the order in which, and the very second at which, they were to be offered; while Mr. David Dudley Field personally handed certain of them to the leading performers, with further verbal instruction. Early the next morning there took place one of the most remarkable comparisons of watches on record. A special messenger visited the Dudley Observatory, and obtained the exact time, which was by him communicated to every active performer in the approaching farce; or, rather, to all except the vulgar majority, to whom time was of no consequence, they being hired by the day, and constituting the fierce democracy of the occasion. These gentlemen arrived by the morning train from New York; they were a very singular party, such as is more frequently seen in the neighborhood of the riotous election precincts of New York City than in the offices of respectable corporations. A breakfast was negotiated for them by an employee of the Fall River line of steamers, which constituted "Admiral" Fisk's naval command, at the saloon in the station; and there they stood and fed at the counter, as rough a set of patriots as ever stuffed a ballot or hit from the shoulder. Some of them had coats, and some had not; their clothes were in various stages of dilapidation, as also were their countenances; open shirts disclosed muscular breasts, and rolled-up trousers stockingless feet; one man saved himself the trouble of rolling up both legs of his trousers by having only one; they emphatically belonged to that class technically known as "roughs," a class subsequently defined by a witness as "men with scarred faces and noses, and black eyes." Under the

178

circumstances it was little to be wondered at, that, while they indulged in a "square meal," the keeper of the saloon gave directions to have his silver counted. Pending the feeding of the democracy, their proxies were in course of preparation; at last all was ready, and between eleven and twelve o'clock they were marched up fifty strong to the offices of the company.

Everywhere things proceeded exactly according to plan. On his way in a carriage to the corporation offices, Mr. Shearman happened to see the injunction of Judge Clerke served on two of the three inspectors as they were on their way to the meeting. This settled two points; the injunction was a surprise; and the regular inspectors were disposed of. Judge Barnard's more important order was meanwhile sent to the sheriff, and the messenger was specially instructed by Mr. Shearman himself to hand it to him with this Roman injunction, "Sheriff, do your duty!" This instruction was given at nine o'clock, but, curiously enough, the official had to consult his lawyer about the service of the process, and this lawyer happened to be one of Mr. Fisk's numerous legal advisers; with that gentleman he remained in counsel until half past eleven o'clock, when at last he was advised to make his arrests at once. By this time all the parties were collected at the offices of the company. It might fairly be called a mixed society. Mr. Van Valkenburg had tendered to the Governor's receivers a guard of men from the shops of the road, but these had been refused, and a large force of Albany police were on duty in the building. Some thirty of the employees of the company were on hand against an emergency, but under positive orders not to enter the offices until sent for. Up stairs was a large array of stockholders, directors, real and contingent, a few receivers, and a score or two of counsel. Then came the New York importation of ruffians, who were divided into squads under the command of divers officials of the Fall River boats, the Erie Railway and the Grand Opera House; thus marshalled, and each man proxy in hand, they were marched into the room and formed in line at one end of it. Besides these there was present a choice collection of Albanians of somewhat similar character, either neutrals or inclined to Mr. Ramsey. How they got there did not appear, but if the instructions to the police to allow no one but holders of certificates of stock to pass up stairs were enforced that day, these certificates were certainly held by a great many strange characters. The Erie party, prominent among whom were Messrs. David Dudley Field, Thomas G. Shearman, and James Fisk, Jr., took possession of the directors' room, which their assortment of "New York stockholders" wellnigh filled; in the adjoining room were Messrs. Ramsey, Pruyn, and their friends and advisers.

Exactly at fifteen minutes before twelve o'clock, by observatory time, one Colonel North, to whom that *rôle* in the Erie parts had been assigned, moved the organization of the meeting. No opposition was encountered, and the gentleman cast for the part of chairman was duly installed. The resolve indorsed "No. 1, Immediate," was then recited by Colonel North, Mr. Shearman standing at his side watch in hand, and the old inspectors were voted out of office and the new ones in. The officers thus elected at once retired to the treasurer's room, where the poll was to be held, whither they were immediately followed by Mr. Shearman, still watch in hand; having satisfied himself that all was in readiness there, this master of ceremonies immediately returned to the side of Colonel North and resumed his comparison of timepieces. At last he said: "It is now one minute of twelve; keep your watch open and be sure that you offer these resolutions at a little after twelve, and not before; and, in order to make sure, wait a few seconds after twelve, but not more than fifteen seconds." With this parting injunction he left the Colonel to his own devices, and "at thirty seconds of twelve" returned to the inspectors' room, just in time to find an injunction served on those officials. It was issued on the complaint of David Groesbeck, and enjoined an election unless the stock held by him was first voted on. Now, at last, was developed the entire significance of the *ex parte* order under which Mr. William J. A. Fuller was made receiver of this stock. There were twenty-five hundred shares of it; Mr. Groesbeck had paid for several hundred of them; he was at that very moment in the next room; he was on every ground bitterly opposed to the Erie direction, and to the parody of an election then in process; Mr. William J. A. Fuller was the receiver of the stock, and it was to this receiver, now conveniently standing at his elbow, that Mr. Shearman turned and remarked: "An injunction has been served restraining this election from going on, unless the votes on the twenty-four hundred shares which you hold are first received, and you had better vote." Thus appealed to, Mr. Fuller modestly replied that he had not intended to vote at this election, but, having been appointed receiver, he deemed it his duty to do all in his power to preserve the property, and concluded his statement by giving as a reason for his vote that the ticket which he offered was composed of men of the highest character and ability, whose election would best secure the rights of all parties to the litigation. At the close of these remarks he actually voted, and the curious spectacle was exhibited of a court of equity taking a man's stock away from him on the ground that it was illegally issued and could not be voted on at all, and then proceeding to vote on it itself, before the man's face and against his wishes. Viewed calmly, and after the event, such a proceeding strikes one chiefly as an extremely droll joke. The climax of the humorous, however, was not attained until some months later, when Mr. Fuller gravely stated in court that, as a receiver, he considered it his duty to vote on stock without consulting the wishes of its ostensible owner, and that for his services as receiver in this case he had as yet received no remuneration, but expected the regular fees, amounting to $15,000. After Mr. Fuller had thus relieved Mr. Groesbeck of the trouble of voting, and after the meeting in the next room had gone through a nominal reorganization to meet the letter of the law, the polls were declared open. The inspectors were withal curiously careless, or too intent on the passage of time to think of aught else; they certainly neglected to be qualified by taking oath as to the performance of their duties, which was specially prescribed in the by-laws; neither did they use any ballot-box, other than the straw hat of one of their number. In this, however, the ballots were deposited, and the election went briskly on for some fifteen minutes, when, under the names of John Doe, Richard Roe, and James Jackson, the inspectors were again enjoined, this time from any further proceedings. Most of their tickets had, however, already been voted, and this injunction was violated by the reception of others, subsequently offered, only in a moderate degree.

Meanwhile events did not stand still in the little library adjoining the directors' room, where Mr. Ramsey and his friends were collected. The sheriff of Albany, after leaving the office of his legal adviser, proceeded to "do his duty." As Mr. Ramsey was intently listening in the president's office to Colonel North, who was moving the organization in the next room, some one suddenly touched his arm, and he became conscious of the sheriff at his side. Here was a thunderbolt. At the very instant when his presence was most necessary, when all depended on the full possession of his liberty and his faculties, he found himself, the secretary of the company and its legal adviser, under arrest. The thing could not have been better timed. To understand the full possible effect of this move, it is necessary to bear in mind a remark made by Mr. Shearman in his subsequent testimony, though in another connection: "I didn't want to lose a second's time, because I knew the value of time in this case, and I knew that the whole question would have to depend upon the question of which meeting was organized first." The officials of the road were therefore arrested, by mere accident, as it was claimed, just when they should have been organizing their meeting. Nor did the possible benefit to be derived from this measure stop here. The election was limited to one hour, and the sheriff was instructed "to do his duty." He might have effected his arrest at ten o'clock; but had he done so, the parties would have been bailed at once, and the arrest might as well not have been made. Having been made at exactly the right moment, the sheriff might now further construe it to be his duty to remove the prisoners to his office, there to arrange their bail. The votes on which Mr. Ramsey relied were, of course, held by him in the usual form of proxies; they were, in fact, on this day so cast by him. Could he, therefore, be held in durance, away from the offices, by any fictitious delays and objections, for one short hour, the election would be over and irrevocably decided against him. The construction the sheriff should give to "his duty" in the premises was very vital, and fully warranted his lengthy interview with that gentleman who was the common adviser of himself and the Erie Railway Company. The whole proceeding certainly spoke volumes for the ingenuity and resource of those who engineered it. In its style it could not have been improved.

Mr. Ramsey was thus a prisoner. He proposed at first to leave the room to consult his friends, but was requested by the sheriff to remain in it, and here he was soon visited by Mr. David Dudley Field, of counsel for the Erie Railway Company, who satisfied himself that the sheriff was doing "his duty" by taking a comprehensive glance at the situation. Finding this greatly to his mind, he then proceeded, with a smile indicative of profound satisfaction and with his thumbs in the armholes of his waistcoat, to inquire of Mr. Ramsey as to the present condition of his health. Mr. Ramsey has the reputation of being a remarkably cool and imperturbable man, so that now, when his counsel, Mr. Smith, entered the room in a state of intense excitement and indignation, and also under arrest, he received simply a direction to go back and attend to the election, while Mr. Ramsey himself effected the bail arrangements. It is not clear whether the sheriff lacked nerve to construe his duty as he might have done, or whether the delay already occasioned was considered sufficient; at any rate, though he certainly arrested his prisoners at exactly the proper moment, he did not remove them from the building. He was, indeed, even provided with blank bail bonds, which were produced and filled, though not until objection had been made to the security of one or two gentlemen notoriously worth millions; and this done the prisoners were released. All this had occupied half an hour; on the theory of Mr. Shearman it was now too late, the moment had passed; the *coup* had been completely successful. Mr. Smith had, indeed, gone back and organized a stockholders' meeting in the hall of the building; but not until ten minutes after twelve, and when the polls of the other organization had been long open. The Erie party were, in their own belief, in possession of the Albany & Susquehanna Railroad beyond a peradventure.

Before going on with the narrative, a few words may here be not out of place concerning the much-discussed question of the limits, if there be any, of the duty which counsel owe to their clients. The celebrated dictum of Lord Brougham in this regard is sufficiently general in its terms: "An advocate, by the sacred duty which he owes his client, knows, in the discharge of that office, but one person in the world, THAT CLIENT AND NONE OTHER. To save that client by all expedient means, to protect that client at all hazards and costs to all others, and among others to himself, is the highest and most unquestioned of his duties; and he must not regard the alarm, the suffering, the torment, the destruction which he may bring on any other. Nay, separating even the duties of a patriot from those of an advocate, and casting them, if need be, to the wind, he must go on reckless of the consequences, if his fate it should unhappily be to involve his country in confusion for his client's sake!"

Certainly no counsel could have acted more fully up to both the letter and spirit of this famous rule than did Messrs. David Dudley Field and Thomas G. Shearman, of counsel for the Erie Railway Company, on this notable occasion. They even "cast to the wind" the single faint limitation conveyed by Lord Brougham in the words "to *save*" and "to *protect*" by all "expedient means"; and, in the intense fervor of their devotion to their clients, had recourse in aggressive proceedings to processes of law which were subsequently judicially characterized as procured "in aid of fraudulent purposes." Attending one's clients to corporation meetings, at the head of a band of "rude, rough, and dangerous persons" and there acting as the master of ceremonies, through the parody of an election, was a case which undoubtedly Brougham would have included in his definition, had it occurred to him; but it probably escaped his notice, from the fact that, since the fall of the Roman Republic, such proceedings have not been usual. The ingenious device, also, of arresting one's opposing counsel and holding him to $25,000 bail, at the moment when his professional services are likely to become peculiarly necessary, is a feature in legal amenities with which the English barrister could not have been expected to be familiar. A high authority has now, however, established these as part of the duties of the American advocate. Instances of similar devotion will, therefore, unless the now obsolete practice of disbarring should chance to be revived, probably hereafter become more common than they hitherto have been. The use of unusual processes of court, unpleasantly suggestive of *lettres de cachet,* quietly procured and suddenly brought in play, would seem also to have met of late with an undeserved odium. Whether these will again arrive at the great efficiency as an element in litigation which they once attained in France will, perhaps, depend upon the degree of fidelity with which sheriffs do their duty. For the shortcomings of such officials, advocates naturally cannot be held accountable, even by the most exacting of clients. The client, moreover, in whose defence Brougham was prepared, if need be, "to involve his country in confusion" was the Queen of England; which, indeed, cannot but cause the deeper sense of a professional devotion, no less reckless, exerted in furtherance of the schemes of Mr. James Fisk, Jr.[4]

[4] It ought, perhaps, to be stated in this connection, that the opinion commonly entertained of the transactions with which the names of Fisk and Gould are associated was not apparently shared by their counsel. These gentlemen, whose close acquaintance with the facts in the case must certainly have qualified them to form an intelligent judgment, have made no concealment of what that extra professional judgment was. Upon this point Mr. Shearman expressed himself very explicitly before a legislative committee at Albany on the 31st of March, 1870, six months subsequent to the Susquehanna proceedings. He then paid the following high tribute to himself and to Messrs. Field, Fisk, and Gould:—

To return from this abstract digression to the narrative, little remains to be said of the election after the release of Mr. Ramsey was effected. While bail was being procured, and the necessary bonds executed, a second meeting had been organized by Mr. Smith in the hall before the offices, and this meeting had proceeded to choose inspectors, who were duly sworn and received from the secretary the prescribed list of stockholders. They then opened their polls in the same room and at the same desk at which the opposition inspectors were still sitting. Mr. Shearman immediately stepped in front of them and began, on various grounds, to challenge every vote. Of course his challenge was disregarded, but the process was kept up by himself or others, until, towards one o'clock, both polls were declared closed. Neither party attempted to vote at the polls

---

"If I were to speak from my own personal judgment of the management of the (Erie) road, I should say that I have never been able to find where these fraudulent acts charged were committed. I have never been able to find where the villainy comes in. I have been looking for it very anxiously. I have thought that the newspapers were edited by men so much wiser than myself that they must know all about it, and I confess that when I entered upon the service of the company, amid a perfect clamor on the part of the newspapers, I thought they were edited by such wise men that there must be something wrong, and I entered upon my duties with fear and trembling, but I found no occasion for fear and trembling."

Mr. Littlejohn. You are speaking as a lawyer now?

Mr. Shearman. No, sir,—as a man; and now as a lawyer I say that I think it is no slight tribute to the character of the gentlemen who are in the management of the Erie Company, that, knowing as they did how particular I was in regard to the management of its officers, how careful I was that no injustice should be done to the company, and how strongly determined I was that its interests should not suffer, they confided their affairs in my hands. And they have confided also in a gentleman of superior age and of very high character, a gentleman with a Quixotic sense of honor, a gentleman who has never done a dishonorable action, a gentleman whom the other side would have been glad to engage for themselves if they could have done so,—Mr. David Dudley Field. Mr. Field has been chosen by the Erie Railway Company as their adviser, and, trained with Mr. Field, I have learned something of his high sense of professional honor, etc.

of the other, nor was there any disorder or disturbance. The two boards then canvassed their votes; the Erie board declared that the ticket voted for at their polls had received 13,400 votes, and was elected. Shortly afterwards the Ramsey board declared that the ticket voted for at their poll had received 10,742 votes, and was elected. The two boards of directors thus chosen then met and organized, the one by the choice of Colonel Church as president, and the other by the re-election of Mr. Ramsey; and having then sufficiently regarded each other from the opposite sides of the directors' room, in due time they adjourned.

The election was over, and apparently nothing was decided by it. Each of the boards elected claimed to be the regular and only lawful one, and neither of them in any way recognized the other. Fortunately the agents of Governor Hoffman were still in actual possession. The Erie party had, indeed, endeavored to take advantage of this fact, by including in their list of directors both Messrs. McQuade and Banks, who were then operating the road under the authority of the Governor. This move wholly failed. Both of these gentlemen instantly and peremptorily withdrew from the board when notified of their election. Governor Hoffman was the one person now responsible, and he very wisely called upon the courts to decide who was legally entitled to the possession of the road. At his direction the Attorney-General, immediately after the election, began a new suit, in which all parties litigant were included, and a general decision on the merits was prayed for. This was the only way to cut the knot. The previous litigation was in a state of hopeless chaos. Twenty-two suits had been begun, a score of injunctions had been issued, numberless orders had been made, and both parties now stood ready to continue the same style of warfare, just as long as any judge could be found who disregarded the duties of his position on the one side, or who did not lack nerve on the other.

The action brought by the Attorney-General came on for trial before Justice E. Darwin Smith, at Rochester, on the 29th of November succeeding the election. The intervening time had been wasted by neither party. Messrs. Fisk and Gould had utilized it in those manipulations of the gold market, which had resulted in the celebrated explosion of September 24, long to be famous as the "black Friday" in Wall Street annals. Mr. Ramsey, meanwhile, had confined his attention to the quarrel already existing, and had carried the war vigorously into Africa, assailing the Erie management in its own stronghold through the suit of *Ramsey* vs. *Erie et als.* Writs, orders, injunctions, receiverships, and conflicts of jurisdiction had become matters of such daily occurrence as hardly to excite a passing notice, and the complications which had grown up around the Erie ring were only exceeded by the scandal they caused. Hitherto, strong in the protection of the more reckless of the city judges, Messrs. Gould and Fisk had suffered no material defeat; they had, indeed, in so far as the law was concerned, carried all before them; for to them the law was simply a process for annoying others, and obstructing all that was calculated to annoy them. Foiled in their attempt to get control of the Susquehanna road by force, they did, indeed, now try to get it by negotiation; they proposed a compromise of all existing disputes on the basis of a lease of this road by the Erie for a term of ninety-nine years, at a rent equal to seven per cent on its bonds and stock outstanding, with a thirty per cent stock dividend flung in as a bonus. The Susquehanna people listened to the proposal, but it finally appeared that no further guaranty than the word of the Erie managers was contemplated. The Atlantic & Great Western Railroad had already illustrated the value of that. Like Falstaff's tailor, the Susquehanna people "liked not the security"; and the other party, like the fat old knight himself, "had as lief they would put ratsbane in my mouth as offer to stop it with security." The negotiation fell wholly through, and nothing remained but the arbitrament of a country justice of the Supreme Court.

At the end of November the case was in order for trial. The Executive, the Attorney-General, the court, and the Ramsey counsel were ready and in earnest. The usual motions for delay from the other side were received with little favor. It was shown that another suit, in which Messrs. Fisk and Gould and their leading counsel were engaged, was then on trial before Judge Barnard. It was of no avail; the parties were ordered to proceed, and the case before Judge Barnard had to be postponed. The trial lasted ten days, and a vast amount of evidence was put in. Mr. Fisk and Mr. Gould were conspicuous by their absence from the witness-stand, but their counsel were put upon it, and Messrs. Harris and Shearman each told his own story. Some features of the evidence and incidents of the trial were far from creditable. Among these may especially be mentioned an attempt to create an impression that Mr. Ramsey had once been under an indictment for forgery. So grave a charge seemed most unlikely to be made without some shadow of reason. In this case, however, it was wantonly advanced, and even the machinery through which it was manufactured was subsequently exposed. Naturally this proceeding and others reacted violently on those who had sought to derive advantage from them. Public feeling in the court-room and in the city of Rochester grew very strong as the case proceeded, showing itself in ways not to be mistaken. As the case was on the equity side of the court, there was no intervention of a jury, no chance of an inability to agree on a verdict. After the evidence was all in, and the case had been elaborately argued by Mr. David Dudley Field for the Erie party, and by Mr. Henry Smith for the Susquehanna party, Judge Smith took the papers, but reserved his decision. It was January before this was made public.

There are cases where a judge upon the bench is called upon to vindicate in no doubtful way the purity as well as the majesty of the law; cases in which the parties before the court should be made to feel that they are not equal, that fraud is fraud even in a court of law,—that cavilling and technicalities and special pleading cannot blind the clear eye of equity. It is possible that even a judicial tone may be overdone or be out of place. There are occasions when the scales of justice become almost an encumbrance, and both hands clutch at the sword alone. Whether the magistrate upon whom the decision of this cause devolved was right in holding this to be such an occasion is not now to be discussed; it is enough to say that his decision sustained at every point the Ramsey board, and crushed in succession all the schemes of the Erie ring. The opinion was most noticeable in that it approached the inquiry in a large spirit. Its conclusion was not made to turn on the question of a second of time, or a rigid adherence to the letter of the law, or any other technicality of the petti-fogger; it swept all these aside and spoke firmly and clearly to the question of fraud and fraudulent conspiracy. All the elaborate comparison of watches, and noting of fractional parts of a minute, which marked the organization of the Erie meeting were treated with contempt, but the meeting itself was pronounced to be organized in pursuance of a previous conspiracy, and the election held by it was "irregular, fraudulent, and void." The scandals of the law—the strange processes, injunctions, orders, and conflicts of jurisdiction—were disposed of with the same grasp, whenever they came in the path of the decision. The appointment of Fuller as receiver was declared to have been made in a "suit instituted for a fraudulent purpose," and it was pronounced in such "clear conflict with the law and settled practice of the court" as to be explicable only on a supposition that the order was "granted incautiously, and upon some mistaken oral representation or statement of the facts of the case." The order removing the regular inspectors of election was "improvidently granted" and was "entirely void"; and the keeping it back by counsel, and serving it only at the moment of election, was "an obvious and designed surprise on the great body of stockholders." The suit under which the Barnard order of arrest was issued against Ramsey and Phelps was instituted without right, the order of arrest was unauthorized, the order to hold to bail "most extraordinary and exorbitant," and was procured "in aid of fraudulent purposes." The injunction forbidding Ramsey to act as president of the company was "entirely void." The three thousand shares of forfeited stock reissued to Mr. Groesbeck were pronounced "valid stock," and numerous precedents were cited in which the principle had been sustained. Even the subscription for the nine thousand five hundred new shares of stock by Ramsey and his friends, on which they had not even attempted to vote at the election, was declared, in point of law, regular, valid, and binding. Upon the facts of the case the decision was equally outspoken; it was fraud and conspiracy everywhere. "The importation and crowding into a small room" of a large number of "rude, rough, and dangerous persons," and furnishing them with proxies that they might participate in the proceedings of the meeting, "was a gross perversion and abuse of the right to vote by proxy and a clear infringement of the rights of stockholders, tending, if such proceedings are countenanced by the courts, to convert corporation meetings into places of disorder, lawlessness, and riot." Finally, costs were decreed to the Ramsey board of directors, and a reference was made to Samuel L. Selden, late a judge of the Court of Appeals, to ascertain and report a proper extra allowance in the case, and to which of the defendants it was to be paid.

The legal scandals of the case were not yet quite exhausted. No sooner was this decision announced and telegraphed to New York, than the Erie counsel at once had recourse to the judges of that city. As a matter of course, an *ex parte* order was instantly granted, staying the entry of judgment. It reached Rochester a few hours too late; the judgment was entered. The next day a new order was obtained, staying all proceedings under the judgment; and this was served on Messrs. Banks and McQuade, who were still in possession of the road. Recourse was had to Judge Peckham, who quietly declared the stay of no effect, and granted an order putting the Ramsey board in possession. Then at last the keys were delivered to them. The Erie counsel were not yet satisfied. A motion was made to vacate the judgment. This was supported by affidavits of counsel of the most unusual nature. Imputations of unfairness, irregularity, bias, and conduct otherwise wholly unbecoming a magistrate, were advanced against Judge Smith. The four leading lawyers of the defeated party then united in a certificate, which concluded with these singular words: "We have examined the opinion of Mr. Justice Smith in this cause, and, in our judgment, it is in every material part erroneous, either in fact or in law." It may be necessary to mention here that this was a certificate of counsel on the losing side of a decided case, applying to one judge of the Supreme Court of New York, to vacate a judgment just entered by another judge of the same court. It ought to be unnecessary to add that the assumptions on which the motion was based were pronounced "simply monstrous"; and the affidavits were ordered to be stricken from the record as "irrelevant and impertinent." Nothing now remained to the Erie faction but the slow process of appeal, with their opponents in actual possession.

The struggle was over. Long before any action could be taken on the decision of Judge Smith, at the general term of the court, the Albany & Susquehanna Railroad was beyond the reach of Fisk or Gould or the Erie Railway. Early in February, 1870, the Ramsey direction leased the whole property in perpetuity, and on very favorable terms, to the Hudson & Delaware Canal Company. This arrangement transferred the struggle from the comparatively weak shoulders of the railroad itself to those of one of the most powerful and wealthy corporations in the country. With it the Erie managers could not afford to quarrel, so they were fain to profess themselves satisfied with the result, and to desist from the contest.

Meanwhile the Hon. Samuel L. Selden was busy over his reference; and the case was wellnigh forgotten before he made his report. When it was made, it was calculated to revive a very fresh recollection of the litigation in the minds of Mr. Fisk's board of directors. This was composed of thirteen individuals, of whom Messrs. Fisk and Gould were two. The report of Mr. Selden was long and very minutely drawn; it was a document likely to be accepted by the court, and not easily overthrown on appeal. "In view of the whole history of this extraordinary case," and in consideration of the assumption by the Albany & Susquehanna Railroad Co. of the entire expenses of the litigation, the sum of ninety-two thousand dollars was fixed upon as a just and proper extra allowance to be paid by the persons constituting the Fisk board of directors to those persons constituting the Ramsey board.[5]

[5] An appeal was taken by the Fisk board of directors from the decision of Judge Smith, referred to in the text, and reported in 7 Abbot's Pr. Rep. N.S., p. 265. The decision of the General Term was not announced until May, 1871. It turned wholly upon technical points, and in no respect entered into the merits of the controversy; upon these the findings of the court below were apparently accepted as conclusive. The decision of Judge Smith was affirmed in so far as it declared the election of the Fisk board fraudulent and void, and that of the Ramsey board valid, on the ground that this question was properly before the court, and it was competent to pass upon it. Judge Smith had also decreed that the proceedings in all the suits on either side between the parties defendant should be stayed and discontinued. This relief, it was held, upon technical grounds, the court below was not competent to grant, and upon this point the decision was reversed. It was also reversed upon the question of costs, upon the ground that in an action brought by the People against two sets of defendants the court had no power to grant costs to one set against the other.

The Ramsey party was, therefore, sustained in the possession of the property; but the Fisk party escaped the payment of costs under the Selden reference. So far as the scandals in litigation were concerned, which gave so great a notoriety to this case between the preparation and publication of this paper, the court at General Term confined itself to a simple closing reference to them. Profound regret was expressed at the occurrences which had preceded the action then before the court, which in itself, however, it was declared had been marked by no unbecoming conduct on the part of counsel.